"A passionately felt, intelligent, and personal narrative of what it is like to be a mother today and to care about, and to try to make changes in, the entrenched way that men, women, and institutions relate to the daily care of children."—Helen Yglesias, author of *How She Died* and *Family Feelings*.

"Not militant rhetoric, this book . . . documents real events with a certain smile. It is a book to enjoy."—*The Cleveland Plain Dealer*

"The book . . . is witty, perceptive and interesting throughout. . . . This is not just another day-care book: in ways this book is more about adults than about children."—*The Soho Weekly News*

"A spare, modest, beautifully written and funny book. . . . What a loss it would be if only people with kids were to become the audience for this book, because it's a fascinating narrative that, in a deceptively casual way, confronts head-on the contradictions of emotional survival for the non-rich today, specifically, but not at all exclusively, for those who happen to be parents. . . .

"[What Harlow's book] does is to share experience at the highest level of intensity and communicate the excitement—and the terror—of people who are turning their lives around. . . . [It is] terrifically readable and, as all really good books must be, wonderfully disturbing."—Sara Blackburn, *The Real Paper*

"Harlow tells an engaging and lively story that's great fun to read. . . .

"The subtitle of the book is 'Village Child Rearing within the City.' Read 'village' as a psychological place. Read it to mean 'not a children's school at all' but 'a family school.' Read it to mean a community whose common concern was rearing the children, not storing them. They didn't separate their kids from the secure family environment so necessary for healthy development; they extended the family for the sake of child rearing. 'We hadn't separated at all. We had just included more people in the circle of mother and child.' "—Buff Bradley, *Learning Magazine*

Nora Harlow

Sharing the Children

village child rearing within the city

Photographs by Jinx Roosevelt

HARPER COLOPHON BOOKS
Harper & Row, Publishers
New York, Hagerstown,
San Francisco, London

This book is dedicated,
with love,
to Ireane and Myron who raised me,
to Eva and Nora who raised her,
and to Fern who raised him.

A hardcover edition of this book is published by Harper & Row,
Publishers, Inc.

SHARING THE CHILDREN. Copyright © 1975 by Nora Harlow. All rights
reserved. Printed in the United States of America. No part of this book may
be used or reproduced in any manner whatsoever without written permission
except in the case of brief quotations embodied in critical articles and reviews.
For information address Harper & Row, Publishers, Inc., 10 East 53rd
Street, New York, N.Y. 10022. Published simultaneously in Canada by
Fitzhenry & Whiteside Limited, Toronto.

Designed by C. Linda Dingler

First HARPER COLOPHON edition published 1976.

STANDARD BOOK NUMBER:06–090512–3

76 77 78 79 10 9 8 7 6 5 4 3 2 1

Contents

A section of photographs follows page 100

Author's Note

All of the incidents described in this book actually happened, not once or twice to one person, as in the book, but again and again to many people over a period of years. Most of the characters are real people, whose real names are used. The few characters whose names are fictitious are composites representing types of people our group encountered rather often.

1. Women and Children First

My daughter was born in New York City in 1965. She was lonely and cranky and bored stuffed up in an apartment and I was too. Whitney's father worked in an office all day. And there wasn't a grandmother for five hundred miles. There were all these other mothers and babies living within blocks of us, all in apartments in the city with one parent, sometimes two, but we didn't know each other. We were cut off from the rest of the community. This was the way it was supposed to be, one woman and her children, alone.

Whitney was a wonderful baby. She was beautiful. She smiled. She was a happy baby. She said "ma ma" and "da da" and gurgled and cooed. But she was a real baby and slobbered and vomited and cried and cried and cried and cried and she wanted to eat in the middle of the night and then her gums hurt and after her diaper rash was over she got the earache and for years she urinated and defecated any time of the day or night and no matter where she was or what she was doing. She was mine. *All* mine. I hated the every-minute-of-every-day responsibility I was saddled with and the loneliness. A six-year wait to begin life on a part-time basis seemed very long. (Even writing this years later, my chest grows tight with anxiety.)

I loved Whitney but I hated the sandbox life. Her birth had forced me farther into the female world—farther than I wanted to go. I preferred men. They were better thought of, smarter, had more money, had more ease of movement through the society, were more courageous, and taller. I knew how women were—not my mother or my college roommates, but *those* women. They were vain, silly, emotional, superficial, small-minded. The male world —the world, which was difficult enough for me to gain any attention from during college: "Your work is excellent, really excellent,

1

for a girl, that is"—that world had tightened ranks when I sought creative, challenging, well maybe even slightly interesting work. "How fast do you type?" "Be sure to clean the ashtrays."

And now, after years of protestations about how I was different, I found myself the same. That baby separated me from the males. I had only one male friend left, only one friend, period, my husband, Lester, and he knew nothing of birth pains, diaper services, babysitters, colic, or breast-feeding. Lester offered to go through our building, knock on all the doors, and ask if anyone inside wanted to be Nora's friend. We laughed, but it wasn't entirely a joke.

I was unhappy, but defiant. I sat away from *them* at the sandbox, afraid of sinking into their talk of detergents and hamburger recipes, afraid of their rejection when they discovered my male ambitions and my daughter's gray underpants.

And then I met Nancy at a big community meeting, where I was speaking on the evils of institutional expansion and she was looking fine in large sunglasses, floppy hat, and paisley dress. And the children were home, so neither of us knew the other one was just a housewife. People at the meeting were forming committees to organize tenants and to arrange neighborhood safety patrols. Nancy and I found ourselves alone together at the section of the room set aside for the daycare committee. After she talked about her two daughters and I talked about my one daughter we formed ourselves into a committee of two to set up a daycare center for our neighborhood—our neighborhood, which was in turmoil, which might even be gone before our project was completed.

My daughter, my husband, and I were living, and still live, on the upper west side of New York City. Our neighborhood is Morningside Heights, which encompasses the area between Riverside Drive and Morningside Drive from 110th Street to 125th Street.

There were sixteen educational, religious, and medical institutions that already owned most of the neighborhood. Columbia University was the big owner. Having already acquired 80 percent of Morningside Heights, it was rapidly buying up the rest, and with its colleagues carrying out an institutional master plan that was to throw out all the neighborhood families, level the area, and build the largest institutional complex in the world.

The year Whitney was born, we were being evicted. Not just Lester, Nora, and Whitney, but everybody on our block. The families didn't leave without a struggle. Court suits. Picket lines. Demonstrations. Moving vans. The university got to level the block but it was forced to rent apartments in the neighborhood to the last tenants, the fighters. A victory. We were able to continue living in our community. By 1968 more than ten thousand people had been forced out of the neighborhood by the sixteen institutions.

The university had even managed to obtain "air rights" to 3.5 acres of Morningside Park which belonged to Harlem. They wanted to use it to build a gymnasium for themselves and in the spring of 1968 brought heavy machinery into the park, demolished a playground, tore out trees, blasted out natural rock formations, dug an enormous hole, and issued a pamphlet called "Partners in the Park" with pictures of smiling black children all over the cover.

People from the Morningside Heights and Harlem communities protested. Some lay down in front of the machinery and were carted off to jail. The hole got bigger.

It was Columbia students who finally stopped the construction. Hundreds of them marched over to the gym site, tore down the fence, and created such a furor that the institution pulled out the heavy machinery. The students then took over or "liberated" their own school buildings and the battle of Morningside Heights was on.

After a couple of weeks the trustees called in the city police, who beat the students bloody and arrested nearly a thousand. You could hear the screaming all over the neighborhood.

In response community members "liberated" a tenement on 114th Street to protest years of the university's criminal landlord practices and to support the students. After a few hours the trustees called the police. Lester, my husband, and most of my friends and neighbors were arrested. I was home with the baby. When everyone was released from jail we got together and formed a Community Action Committee and held a big open meeting at Corpus Christi Church and that's where I met Nancy, and where we formed our daycare committee.

The first official meeting of our daycare committee was held at a playground in Riverside Park and was also attended by Whitney, Hagar, and Bootsie. Whitney was already three. Bootsie was two and Hagar was four.

Nancy and I had been in awe of each other from the beginning because we were the two people out of that large meeting who said confidently that we would start a daycare center for the community. Questionnaires had been filled out at the door and their checks indicated that daycare was number two on the list of what the community wanted, after safety. The whole evening there were waves of emotion circulating through the crowd, the people there had been in jail, had been evicted, had been in landlord-tenant court, had gone without heat and hot water, had fought the institutions or were willing to fight. Men were organizing safety patrols and tenant committees, and there were Nancy and I holding the questionnaires and feeling the world was in our favor.

In the deserted park playground the world seemed larger and harder to live in. Our project overwhelmed us. We didn't have any place to put a daycare center. There were hundreds of vacant apartments and storefronts in our community, but they were being hoarded by the institutions and we couldn't rent them even if we had money to pay the rent, which we hadn't. We also had no money to pay salaries for staff. Daycare centers were budgeted at $2,500 to $3,000 per child, which meant we needed about $100,000 for a small center. We didn't have any money to pay even part of our child's share because we weren't working.

Even if we did manage to rent a space suitable for children and raise $100,000, there was the bureaucracy to cope with. The city officials had written thousands of rules governing daycare and it would take a long time to learn them and three or four years to comply with them and get approval from all the city agencies like the Bureau of Child Health, the Buildings Department, and the Fire Department. And neither Nancy nor I wanted to be like the woman we had read about in the *New York Times'* "food, family, fashion, furnishings" page who was being praised for setting up an official daycare center with a license and everything in just four years and on the day it opened her son was seven and going off to second grade at the local public school.

The *Times* writer was astonished that a mere housewife had managed to do it at all. Women with young children just didn't set up daycare centers. That's why there were so few. Men in city government and men looking for business profits set up daycare centers. Women were too busy with their children.

Nancy and I identified with that woman. The more we talked, the more we kept our eyes on the children, the more we saw each other as mere housewives, and the awe each of us felt for the other one began to slip away. We were just regular people, less than regular now that we had the babies. In fact we had been raised in similar families, grew up with similar aspirations, and got married about the same time. My father came out of a mining town in West Virginia and made shovels in a factory for forty years. Her father came off a Wisconsin farm and worked as a minor civil service clerk. Our mothers worked raising children and from time to time at low-paying jobs to help out with the finances. I made it through a state college. Nancy took some courses in fashion design and we both came looking for work in the big city. I was going to work as an actress until my first plays were produced and she was going to be a fashion designer. But jobs as secretaries were all we could get, and so we worked at that until the babies were born and then stayed in our apartments. And Hagar and Bootsie's father was black so there were no visits or packages from their grandparents in Wisconsin.

By this time, when Nancy and I talked about our former aspirations, we would speak apologetically or we dismissed them. She was Hagar and Bootsie's mommy. I was Whitney's mommy and the grocer didn't recognize me when I came in alone.

Now here we were, two housewives sitting on a park bench going over the same daycare material again and again and getting nowhere. Our children behaved well. They liked Riverside Park. Once they even let us alone for ten whole minutes. But one of them was always falling down, and Bootsie tried to get on the big swing by herself, and Whitney wanted me to watch her on the slide every time, and there was a fight. By the time we got down to working out a plan, or rather failing to work out a plan, all of our children wanted to sit on our laps. There had been two major crying sessions and after two more, and one case of wet pants, we adjourned.

Two more meetings and we were still nowhere. All our thoughts on daycare centers led to a dead end. A daycare center is an institution and we didn't really want to put our children in an institution. Institutions are no place for grownups and certainly detrimental to children. We wanted to do something for women and children like ourselves and a daycare center was what you did when you wanted to do something. We couldn't perceive an alternative. You either put your child in a daycare center, hired a full-time babysitter and paid her most of your salary, or stayed home. And what if you wanted to go to school and there wasn't any salary, only debts? The admissions officer at our neighborhood center admitted that one of their children's mothers was working on her doctorate, but quickly added that they didn't like to take that kind of person. In fact, if there wasn't any salary or you didn't already have eight children most centers wouldn't look at you *or* your child.

A daycare center was an institution where poor children could be left so their mothers would be able to work out of the home from nine to five, Monday through Friday. Hours were tailored to the employer's need, and the price of admission to the low wages paid to female employees. All the mothers paid something, because the theory was that they would appreciate institutional child care more if they bought it, even if their salaries were so low that they could afford to pay only fifty cents a week.

The government or some social agency usually ran the centers, and even when there was a private administrator the government made most of the rules and picked up most of the expenses, keeping budgets as low as possible.

Our center was going to be more humane, run by the community, and cozier, but essentially the same: set up to meet the needs of the business world. We kept trying to fit ourselves and our children into that structure, to follow those rules, and to adjust our lives to those kinds of needs, like all the daycare projects that had gone before. The whole idea was rotten, but great numbers of women had to work out of the home, and were fighting each other trying to get their children into these institutions. For them, a daycare center was a lifesaver. And we couldn't think of anything else so we kept pushing in that direction. But it seemed as if we couldn't get there from here. There was no route. The problems as defined by everybody else were physical space, funding, and a license. These problems were stupendous and we didn't have any connections into that world. We didn't know any directors on any boards or any officials at any funding agencies; we couldn't even get enough time away from Whitney, Hagar, and Bootsie to have a decent meeting. And we couldn't wait years anyway.

Practically there wasn't much to work with. Our only asset: mothers and children and more mothers and children. Not much of an asset. Motherhood kept most of the women in the neighborhood cloistered with their children, and Nancy and I needed allies.

Out of absolute desperation Nancy and I came up with our first independent thought. We decided to stop meeting and planning and to do it. The community needs were specific. We needed something that was ready to operate tomorrow, right here in the neighborhood, that was free, that was available all day Monday through Friday, and that was more like a home than an institution. So Nancy and I started trying to figure out what we could do ourselves right now, like today or tomorrow, just with what we had.

Hmmmmm. Blank. I said that I could take Hagar and Bootsie at my house, and Nancy could take Whitney, but what we really needed was a third woman who would take all three children for an extended time so that Nancy and I could be free to work on the daycare project. That was the perpetual vicious circle, that we needed daycare for our children so that we would have enough time and energy to set up a daycare center for our children.

The third woman was the key. Someone who would take all the children. Flashbulbs went off in our heads. I could take the children for a day. Nancy could take the children for a day. The third woman could take them for a day. And at that point we would already have three-day-a-week daycare for the children. We could start with that, and then keep filling up the week with more women and children until we had daycare nine to five, Monday through Friday. That's all we needed: women and children.

Instead of each woman staying home all the time with one or two children, she would mother five, six, or seven children one day a week and have four free days to work, to go to school, to stop the evictions, to stop the war, to set up daycare centers, to read books, to go to the movies, to play her guitar.

Our children could have steady playmates and even friends, and we could get out of our apartments and back into the world for thirty-two hours a week. We could walk down the street and nobody would even know we were mothers. They would think we were just people.

The staff and the enrollment were automatic. Physical space. We would use what we had: our apartments and the parks and other public places of the city. Money. There was nothing to pay for. Each family's own personal space and belongings would be shared with that day's visitors so there was no rent and no cost for materials. We were free. Regulations! We didn't need any.

Nancy spread the word around the sandboxes and seven or eight women and all their children met in my apartment on a Thursday in late August of 1968, made a few decisions, gathered the children together, and started sharing the following Monday. There was no nonsense.

Decisions were simple and swift. We would meet the needs of the mother and child, not just the business community. Bootsie was included, though she was a full year younger than the other children, because it wouldn't do Nancy much good to have Hagar out of the house if Bootsie were still home. So we forgot about actual age as a criterion and just agreed that to be in the group a child should be able to walk pretty well and should be toilet trained or at least able to stay in her diaper through a session, so the mother for the day wouldn't have to change diapers. Many of the women needed half-a-day child care so we decided on two major sessions a day. Hours: nine to one and one to five. Each woman was responsible for a particular half day or full day a week, and if she or her children were sick she would just trade days with another woman and notify everybody that there was a change. With none of us working full time at paid jobs we could trade days fairly easily. The children were to bring their own lunches. Lunch in the morning. Naps in the afternoon.

The children were Whitney and Kelley, who stayed all day, Hagar and Bootsie and Philip and Phoebe, who were with the group in the morning, and Lisa, who stayed in the afternoon. We had room for more children in the afternoon and every woman there knew three interested mothers so that was no problem.

The children's mothers were the hardiest, most independent, or most desperate women in the neighborhood.

Philip's mother, Kathy, had been arrested in the community-student turmoil and was worried about having to serve the threatened prison term. Kelley, mother of Little Kelley, was waiting for her husband to get out of Columbia Law School so she could start on her own law degree. Phoebe's mother, Jinx, had twins in diapers and Phoebe needed some time out of the house with friends her own age. Lisa's mother, Kay, had worked with children and teenagers in community centers for years. Kay was waiting for her daughter to get older so she could take courses to get licensed to teach in the public schools.

Getting Kelley involved had been a real coup. She was a strong woman, competent, intelligent, and great at organization. And most important, as a graduate-student wife who lived in the graduate-student building, she had access to, and had helped set up, a basement playroom for children on 112th Street, with little tables and chairs and dollhouses and puzzles. The basement playroom was a perfect start. It was still used by graduate-student wives but was mostly empty. Kelley arranged for us to use it every day from one to five. Twelve children could run freely there. Great. More families. And Nancy and I had an ally.

It was so easy. Instant daycare. And it encompassed nearly all our goals. It was free. Community-controlled. Everybody who had the time and energy could join. No bureaucracy. The hours were purposely nine to five to allow all of us at least to become economically independent. The staff, us, had years of experience, were highly motivated, and quite used to listening to three-year-olds.

Kelley made a list of each woman's name, address, phone number, and the portion of the week she worked with the children. The list was all the organization we needed for a year. *Fine.*

The first weeks were rough. Switching from one mother to many mothers meant changes. Separation anxiety. The children cried. The mothers worried. Each woman and child had been together for two or three or four years—the total lifetime of the child—and separating wasn't easy. Mother-and-child. One being. Guilt.

Whitney was one of the criers and I was one of the guilty.

She wanted to play with her new friends but she wanted me to stay by her side while she played. And I did, but it was never long enough and she needed one more kiss and one more hug and then she would cry. Once Nancy lit candles at nine A.M. in her darkened dining room because that was Whitney's favorite thing. Seeing the fire and all the children clamoring for turns at blowing out the candles, she was kind of mesmerized and could hardly remember to cry.

But I could never slip away while she was happy. I hung around to say good-bye again so she would know I was going. And the wails would start. It wasn't just that I wanted my daughter to trust me. Illogically I wanted Whitney to pat me on the back and tell me it was all right if we unclutched each other a little.

But it was never going to happen. Whitney was a baby, thirty inches tall, just three, and without even the semblance of bravado. All I ever got out of her was a very wet kiss. I would put her in the arms of Nancy or Kelley or Kathy or Jinx and walk briskly out the door. Then I would wait in the hall listening to the crying. Listen all the way down in the elevator. Guilt. What was I doing, abandoning my child? I felt terrible.

I was having an identity crisis. I was female. Female *is* mother.

All the males said so. And the older females echoed them. I had received that information in different forms every day for the twenty-seven years of my life and I got the message. This is why, despite all my powers of logic, here I was, an adult woman, listening at doors with a nervous stomach and depression about to set in, all because I had decided to separate from my daughter for 32 hours a week, which only left us 136 hours a week to be together. I was suffocating being all mother. I was scared to death not to be.

The conditioning was frightening. I saw it in Whitney already. She was all girl and she had all the information about her sex and what she was to do lodged somewhere in her brain by the time she was three. She may have known earlier but that was the first year she could express it.

That year she decided—after a few hours in a hospital getting shots, being force-fed wretched medicine, and throwing up quarts, including a lot of baby aspirin—that she wasn't ever going to have babies, and she wasn't going to be a mother ever, ever, ever. I decided the same thing at eight when my tonsils came out, so I understood.

"That's O.K., Whitney. You don't have to have babies. Lots of women don't. But it's really too early to decide. When you're grown-up you will probably *want* to be a mother. You don't even have to have your baby in a hospital, you know. You could have it at home in your own bedroom. That's the way all the women used to have their babies."

Whitney didn't even hear me. She was staring off into her own thoughts and then her face broke and great streams of tears rolled down her face.

"But if I'm not a mother what will I be?"

She let out a wail and collapsed on her bed in the extremes of baby anguish. I held her close, felt her sobs, kept holding and talking quietly to comfort her. I can't remember what I said, only what I felt. I felt like every female who has ever thought deep inside she would be single, would be childless.

Double image: I would run off and sit by myself in a corner. I would attack with my fists to avenge my daughter's pain—and my own.

I told the women. They understood.

A group was developing. One child with her arm around a small tearful comrade. And the mothers comforted each other and said it was fine and for God's sake don't stand in the hall listening, let's go have some coffee, and there were phone calls to see how long Whitney or Little Kelley or Phoebe cried after mommy left. Three minutes was about the maximum. It was very disappointing.

But I didn't have time to brood. Losing a little bit of "my own little baby" went with the new responsibility of mothering seven. At nine o'clock Tuesday morning the children came streaming into my apartment, and half of them were in tears. Two- to four-year-olds are fiery emotional creatures. They hit each other and cry a lot and strut their independence. I knew what to do about Whitney, but *their* children. I was nervous and outnumbered. To stop the crying I had to convince each child that there were other adults in the world she could depend on to take care of her besides her own mommy and that I was one of them. They didn't want to believe me.

The first week Little Kelley sat on the floor in her long brown curls and her overalls crying because she had to go to the bathroom and couldn't get her pants unbuttoned. I told her I was a mommy and I would unbutton her pants. That was my job.

"No. *My* mommy!" She was immovable.

Little Kelley was trying to maintain the status quo. One mother and a small dependent self against the rest of the world. A pretty frightening set of circumstances. No wonder there were so many tears.

The telephones kept us in touch and we talked at drop-off and pick-up times and at chance meetings in the neighborhood. Everybody tried to help everybody adjust.

Nancy said to give Bootsie a doll. She was right. Bootsie had a two-year-old passion. She was happy the whole morning with a doll and some doll clothes and if there was a stroller around you couldn't get her shoes on her to go home.

Kathy said Philip was used to his bottle at eleven A.M. But she didn't want to bother me. Besides, he was getting too old. Poor kid. A new place to spend his Tuesdays and he was off the bottle. Cold turkey. So we decided Philip should bring his bottle when he wanted and put it in the refrigerator. He wasn't in an institution yet. And it made me another adult-to-be-relied-on in Philip's world.

We had to face the fact that many two- and three-year-olds just don't like changes. Whatever was happening before was good enough for them even if they didn't like it. Confronted with anything new, they wanted to back up and consider. They needed time.

I asked Nancy and Kelley to call Whitney the night before and tell her what the children were going to be doing at their homes and to ask her to come. She liked that.

Jinx suggested we talk over the next day's schedule with our children the night before, even act it out with dolls. It worked. At bedtime I would tell Whitney everything, whose home she was going to, what children would be there, and with great emphasis about what time she would come back home, who would bring her home, and how she would make that journey. That getting home part was really important to all the children. If a child had been thinking about mommy picking her up all day and the mother with her told her that her mother would appear at five and then it was someone else, even a favorite person—despair, tears.

Mothering a group was hard work, but there were rewards. After I had proven myself by tying a few shoelaces, being scrupulously fair about every child getting a good long turn on the tricycle, reading "The Three Little Pigs" four times in a row without stopping, and giving extra laptime, cookies, and Band-Aids to the truly desperate, all the children stopped crying. And they all called me mommy.

I was a mommy. It was obvious. Here I was in my own home with my own child and she called me mommy fifty times a day so the other children did too. Besides, when they were having troubles and needed a big person to help them, it was the only word they could think of. I liked being mommy to a raft of kids. And this was the only way it was going to happen for me in this overpopulated world. Mommy was that big person who took care of you. The children had five of this kind plus one special: "my mommy." It's impossible to show with the printed word but when they spoke of "mommy" meaning "my-own-every-day-every-night-all-the-time-and-forever-mommy," the word had a different intensity.

Nancy kept saying how she looked forward to being with the children. We needed the children as they needed us. It wasn't being mothers that we hated so much. It was that being a mother at this particular time and particular place meant isolation, meant only being able to use your mind in a very limited way, meant spending years of your life in the company of child minds and child emotions. The structure of the relationship with the child was wrong. Banding together as women with young children, we quickly found that our fears of separation were groundless. We hadn't separated at all. We had just included more people in the circle of mother and child.

2.   Just the Thirty-one of Us:
Surviving the First Six Months

Almost immediately there were more of us. Demi and Constance joined because they lived across the street from the playroom, and they stayed for years. Demi had three children, the oldest seven. The Episcopal church was trying to tear her home down and she was fighting. Constance had two children, two and four. I had a vivid memory of her at an antigym demonstration years ago. She was a big woman, pregnant, and pushing a baby carriage, and she could yell louder than any of us, man or woman. Demi and Constance were eager to get in that afternoon group because they were both still trying to finish their B.A.s.

And then there were five more women: a nurse on the four-to-twelve shift at St. Luke's, a part-time secretary, and three full-time housewives. So we were a group.

Then Constance brought up the question of her friend who was desperate. Blanche had come to New York from San Diego a few years ago, was single, and was the sole support of a young son, Sean. She worked full time at a low-paying sales job and Sean was living in New Jersey with her sister-in-law until she could make arrangements for him. She sent word that she would be happy to work on Saturdays if we would take her son into the group. We immediately decided to have the group run six days a week.

Blanche would work on Saturdays from ten to four. Only three families had a need for child care on Saturdays, but we all wanted to take care of Sean whether our children were there on his mother's day or not. It wasn't fair but it was the beginning of community.

We were thirteen families. Differences in education, experience, outlook. Some women thought the nurseries in the city were fine;

they just couldn't afford them, or the forms and waiting were too long, or the nurseries were too far away or filled with too many people. They needed a place that was cheap and easy. Ours was the cheapest and easiest, and they didn't want to get too involved because they didn't plan to stay.

But we existed. That in itself was an achievement. Enthusiasm was high. We felt good when Blanche brought Sean to live with her. He was at our door every morning at 8:45 and he stayed all day. His need for full-time daycare made us stick to our schedule. We couldn't cancel out because of heavy rain, or because of all the colds going around, or because of headaches—Sean had to be taken care of. He was so sweet. Black hair. Brown eyes. Just learning to talk. All the children loved Sean and so did the mothers. Sean was the first community child, the first child every mother worried about.

Sean needed us. At the ripe old age of two and a half, he never cried. When Blanche left him he didn't seem to notice. He would stay anywhere, do anything you asked, whenever you asked it, and take anybody's hand to go off anywhere. If another child wanted his toy, he just gave it to him.

Each time Sean did anything we would call each other up.

"He seems to know the word 'bathroom.' "

"Sean cried today. Bootsie grabbed his toy and he struggled and cried."

"Hey, he likes puzzles."

"Sean talked this morning."

Blanche seemed pleased, but the rest of us were ecstatic.

Kay or I would save his watery brown finger paintings for Blanche and she would say "Thank you" and then start yelling at Sean about the watery brown spots all over his clothes. Since it wasn't important to most of us that our children be kept clean, we kept forgetting to keep Sean clean. And to make it worse, it always seemed that Sean just naturally got dirtier than the rest of the children.

We had meetings at Kelley's apartment and talked about all the children, and we wanted to talk with Blanche about Sean, especially about whether or not he talked much when he was at her sister-in-law's and if he was just shy, or confused about talking, and what his words for peeing and bm's were, and how we should handle him if he cried. But Sean's mother was the one person who couldn't seem to make it to meetings.

By the end of the first month at least half of us had intense mother feelings for Sean and intense feelings of frustration and anger toward Blanche. Blanche was a small blond woman who carried herself regally and inspired confidence. She was articulate, attractive, well-dressed. Impressive. Although she had little formal education and lived on a small income, she could have passed for an executive. A couple of mothers talked to her privately about her son, his need for extra attention from her, his need for consistent encouragement. She would always take these conversations seriously and leave the mother feeling that everything was going to be much better for Sean now that his mother understood. But it wasn't. Blanche was consistently erratic. She would lavish affection on him when he was bad; she would punish him severely for something a two-year-old couldn't be expected to handle; she would ignore him for long periods of time. Her behavior expressed how she was feeling at the moment—not even how she was feeling about her son, but just how she was feeling all by herself.

Mixed in with our anger and frustration at this woman was a great deal of sympathy. Blanche had an exhausting life: going to work every day, buying the groceries, doing the laundry, feeding Sean, toilet-training him, getting up in the night with him. When she left her downtown job she wasn't coming home to rest, she was coming home to another work shift. She deserved our sympathy. And yet we often wanted to grab her and shake her, shake some sense into her; she was the only mother Sean was going to have and he was being cheated. Sean loved Blanche. Blanche loved him, she kissed him and hugged him and fed him and clothed him and sheltered him and they had first rights to each other.

There was only so much the other mothers could do. Kelley tried to get her to stop hitting him so much. We were all trying to make their lives easier. He stayed with Kelley in the early morning so Blanche could get downtown in time for work and he was at one of our houses after work until Blanche picked him up and sometimes with Kelley and Little Kelley, or with Whitney and me for overnight.

Sean was becoming more and more a child to be reckoned with. Whitney, Hagar, Bootsie, Phoebe, Kelley, Philip, and Lisa were sailing along. It only seemed natural to them to play every day with each other's toys and go off on adventures with each other's mommys. They got up when the sun came up, spent the day with their friends, got special attention from a mommy, and then extra-special attention from their mommy, and went to sleep when it got dark.

For their mothers it was rough going. Change was difficult. We were old and set in our ways. None of us ever got up because the sun came up. We got up because a bell rang and it was 6:30 A.M. or 7:30 A.M. and there were socks to find and breakfast to cook, and worries to worry about, and all kinds of people and things to clean.

We kept telling each other that we would just watch the children and listen to them and use our own experience.

Use our own experience. A necessary skill but not an easy one.

First of all, each woman distrusted her own experiences. And we were certainly uneasy about what someone else in the group might come up with. That's part of the reason we felt it was important to get this group together, get everybody working hard with the children, get everybody deeply into this child-care thing.

Education was the answer.

Several of us really thought that if everyone would just read a few of the same books we could continue on without a problem. So with all the children right in front of us, and half a dozen college educations right behind us, we compiled a long list of books on the absolute-right-way-to-raise-children-once-and-for-all. Kelley and Kathy and Jinx between them owned most of these books and started passing them around. Of course there were at least four women in the group who never read books, period. Furthermore, every single life experience of every woman there was proof that education was not the answer, but we didn't let that stop us.

Nancy and Kay and I had read *Summerhill* and liked it and went out proselytizing. Demi threw *Summerhill* across the room, disgusted at Neill's attitude toward the Catholic church and moral instruction. Jinx and Kelley said *Summerhill* was great, and in the next breath announced that everyone should read *Teaching Baby to Read* also, so we could get serious.

Nancy and Kay and I were aghast. Who were these women and what were they thinking, anyway? Nancy called a friend who was a daycare pro to see if the children would be damaged by being taught to read at two and a half. No. So Nancy said O.K., but she wouldn't read the book. It was important to Jinx and Kelley and we needed them to take care of our children, so we all started teaching our babies to read.

And Kelley said that the public schools were so terrible that we could certainly do better than that. If we really tried, we could get our kids to third-grade level by the time they were six. She was right. We could. If that's the way we wanted to spend our time. Kelley and Jinx and Constance and a few others were excited. Here was a real project after all those boring years changing diapers. Kelley was already making up big white cards with big red letters. MOMMY. TOE. HAND. DADDY. We were off into the professional teacher bit—following the book word for word, passing the cards from woman to woman, and also a big black notebook in which we recorded the children's progress.

Teaching babies to read was the kind of task that would separate the women from the girls. The work was hard—especially since Sean could hardly even talk yet and Bootsie spoke her own language, understood by only blood relatives and a few close friends. And there were those studies that said it was doubtful if children that age had the visual capacity to distinguish words at all. Kelley made the letters ten inches high like the man said, and we went on with it.

The first entries in the black book were enthusiastic. All the children learned the MOMMY card right away. Bloody little geniuses. But we always knew that.

A few of the children learned the HAND card right away—and then progress stopped. None of the children was learning anything and we had serious doubts as to whether they ever had learned anything in the first place beyond the fact that it made a lot of women happy if you said MOMMY when they held up a white card with red Magic Marker marks on it. It wasn't a total loss.

We did learn which of our children had the most propensity for cheating, which were the most devious, and which could trick the grownups the most and the longest. My daughter memorized the cards. The one with the dirt spot is TOE; the one with the bent corner is DADDY. Constance's son would say very quickly MOMMY-DADDY-TOE-HAND to every card and then go back to building things. Philip, whose mother, Kathy, was soon to be a college professor, showed the most independence. He would sit on the floor with his bottle and football helmet, look very intellectual, and say, "No." Sean and Bootsie would argue over whose MOMMY was on the card and punch each other and cry. Finally Constance's son, Edmund, organized the children to scream MOMMY-DADDY-TOE-HAND over and over every time they saw any card.

Jinx and Kelley suggested we stop.

And there were mumblings that maybe certain other books on our reading list were probably just as effective. We dropped the reading project, but we kept the black book.

I liked the black book. Each woman wrote about what the children did on her day and how they were feeling and what she did with them and how *she* was feeling, and we passed it from woman to woman and the fathers read every word, sometimes twice if it was about their child.

It was a bit of a comedown, giving up serious academic pursuits. We hurled epithets at ourselves. The major one was "babysitter." What a rotten thing to call a woman. "O.K. Are we *really* doing something with the children or are we just *babysitting*?"

There *was* learning. They learned the days of the week before other children their age. Monday is Jinx's day. Tuesday is Nora's day. Wednesday is Nancy's day. Thursday is Kathy's day. Friday is Kelley's day.

The children learned to help each other taking off shoes and then finding them in their hiding places. They learned to hold hands crossing the street and to wait for everyone and the green light and the mother before one foot was off the curb and to sit fairly quietly in a bus and to wait for Bootsie.

And they wouldn't leave any of us alone. What's a tuba? Read me a story. Can I sew? Can we go to a forest? To the playground? Write my name. Write my daddy's name. Mommy's name. Can I wash the dishes? Can I wash Bootsie? How old will I be on my birthday? How many is that? How old will Whitney be? Hagar? Phoebe? And how old the year after that? And the year after that? And the year after that?

It was confusing. There was nothing for us to hold onto. No slot to fit ourselves into. We weren't babysitting. We certainly weren't *just* mothers. Heaven forbid. And we weren't teachers. We hadn't passed any tests in early education, and some of us hadn't passed any tests in anything. About every six weeks one woman or another would get nervous. What am I doing in this group, anyway? Nobody does this kind of thing with her children —bundling them off every day to a different person's care. Luckily, we rarely hit that anxiety level at the same time. And there was the very practical matter that we were taking care of the children.

The group as a whole had settled into more mundane worries, like how to get through the day. Group child care was hard work.

I had to adapt a lot and to remember things like not filling juice glasses up to the top. That was easy. After I mopped the kitchen floor three times the same morning I never forgot again. And I had to remember to start getting everybody ready to go out an hour before time because Bootsie decided she could dress herself all by herself and it took her half an hour to even get discouraged and I had to remember to tie double knots in shoelaces because as I was tying the fifth pair, I would see the third pair back off somebody's feet and it was too discouraging. And for a while I had to have seven of everything in the same size and shape and color to prevent fights.

I still couldn't manage to get seven little children from my apartment on 119th Street down to the basement playroom on 112th Street through all the city noise and construction and heavy traffic without being in a continual sweat, trying to hold seven hands at once and worrying myself into exhaustion. They would hold onto Bootsie's stroller and that was a help. But sometimes they fought over handle positions and Little Kelley kept stepping on Philip's heels. Sean was always carrying something or other and then he would drop it, usually in the middle of the street.

Billy's mother, who lived on 118th Street, volunteered to meet me on her corner and walk down to the basement playroom every Tuesday and I would walk Billy home when the afternoon group was over.

Kelley decided that we should cook lunch for the children. It was easier than enduring the fighting, and pulling beastly children off of squished-up pieces of private chocolate cake.

Kelley got Jinx to agree to feed all seven on her day, made three phone calls to give out that line about a good hot meal which none of us could resist, and the next day the children were fed hot soup, sandwiches, and milk. No tears, no fights, an occasional substitute food for one that was disliked, and lots of leftover bread. Throwing out half a loaf of bread after every meal was stupid so we just stopped sandwiches altogether and fed them mostly soup, milk, juice, fruits, vegetables, and the insides of sandwiches—sliced meat, cheese, bacon, lettuce, peanut butter on celery, jelly on crackers.

The children wanted to help and if lunch had to be started at 9 A.M. so they could all have five turns doing something or other, that was all right.

Jinx made applesauce with them on the floor in the twins' bedroom because there wasn't enough room for everyone in the kitchen. She got out her meat grinder and had the children grinding up leftover turkey and all kinds of vegetables to make turkey soup and she bought some beef and they all made their own hamburgers from scratch. On my day, I was right in there with my tap water and condensed soup and everybody got a stir.

The grownups relaxed a bit and we stopped trying to force each other into some kind of mold. We came around again to our original premise that each woman should take care of all the children just as she did her own. Many models for the children.

Being ourselves with the children was great for each woman when she was in charge on her day, but it was hard letting go of your child on those other women's days.

Demi trudged up to the campus on an errand in the pouring rain with the whole brood behind her. She said a little water never hurt a child. The children thought this was great. And half the mothers laughed, but half the mothers didn't laugh at all.

Kay said she liked to do artwork with them but she just couldn't get down on the floor and roll around. She didn't have to. Constance did that kind of thing all the time. Constance would bundle various children up in an old mail sack, throw them over her back, cart them around for a while, and then deliver them to each other as presents. And if the children were really good she would pretend she was an antelope frolicking through the forest and they would be tigers and chase her and eat her. Whitney hated to miss a day.

Whitney was walking around singing songs I had never heard, and using expressions I never used. I took her off to the Museum of the City of New York to see the dollhouses and she said she liked the place because she had been there lots of times with Kathy and once with Jinx. It was hard to absorb. There were all these people contributing to Whitney's world and not just me.

I was grateful.

It wasn't daycare like in the books. We weren't mothers like in the books. We weren't perfect people. And thank God, none of us had to be *everything* to our children anymore.

We stayed close to the children.

The adults weren't so close to each other. We weren't alike and we weren't ever going to mesh perfectly together. But we didn't have to. Self-determination. We talked a lot about it. Everybody had at least one friend in the group and we left it at that.

We had one strong bond: the children. We stayed close to the children and that helped our group survive.

I put them all right into dramatic training. "The Three Little Pigs." Twelve performances in an hour and a half. We had to have twelve performances so that everybody got to be the wolf at least twice. Whitney built her house of straw and then ignored the story completely and asked the wolf to come right in. Well, Sean *was* her friend and he was so gloriously happy running all over the room being a wolf that he didn't care about the story either. Little Kelley was upset. She wanted to be in the play, but she wanted everybody to use the exact words of the book and she wanted to use the exact words herself but she couldn't remember them. So she hovered over the actors with her eyes shining with excitement for about seven performances and then plunged in, with a lot of huffs and puffs and chinny-chin-chins.

Kathy had been a professional dancer before Columbia graduate school, the English Department, and motherhood. She had them all marching around the living room clapping out rhythms. But nobody had much staying power, except Hagar, who could have gone on forever and never missed a beat. They all loved to dance and they danced all the time at everybody's house. But Hagar was exceptional. She could really dance, and her dancing was all her own.

Jinx took all the children up on the roof of her building to see the Hudson River, water tanks, chimneys, Little Kelley's house, Riverside Park, and the sky.

Every woman did something or other with numbers and letters and squares and triangles. Sean was obsessed with puzzles. Though all the children were going through a puzzle stage. After the first two weeks Kelley and I were totally bored, but the children kept asking for more puzzles. Sean could do five-piece puzzles, then eleven pieces, and he kept asking for more and didn't want help, even if he couldn't figure it out at all. He finally did it: a twenty-four-piece puzzle.

More women wanted to join but the group was closed. It had been closed for months. Seven children in the morning cared for by one woman. Twelve children in the afternoon cared for by two women. Kelley and I had our daughters in the group from nine to five and worked one full day and Blanche worked Saturdays from ten to four.

Working women desperately needed daycare. That fact haunted us. Our group included only one working woman with a single child: Blanche and Sean. We needed more space. There were too few of us and our apartments kept us apart from other people in the neighborhood and even apart from each other.

Renting a storefront would solve our problem but we couldn't because we didn't have any money, which is why we started doing this in the first place. Our neighbor, Columbia University, had storefronts all over the place, vacant and run-down and not for rent, waiting for the demolition squads to tear down more neighborhood and build more institution.

No one was exactly eager to ask Columbia to share anything. I was the most violent on the subject, having been evicted under great duress by that institution, along with thousands of people over the years, and a few neighbors at the time. The experience changed me. I learned a lot about power, and about not having any, and about the value of neighbors. Nobody really had to be convinced. Half of the women in our group had participated in the '68 rebellion on campus and the other half had pushed strollers past the hundreds of police and piles of equipment and heard the screams and seen the blood all over the concrete after the students were beaten and arrested. And we should ask the same twelve men who ordered the bust if they would please share one of their empty storefronts with us?

We decided to go to the church. The one on Broadway with the big red doors about a block from Nancy's house. Presbyterian. They had a bad reputation in the community, but there was a brand-new friendly young minister who was trying to make amends. That was the word in the neighborhood.

The friendly young minister showed Nancy an enormous room that was never used.

She told him all about our group and how we really needed a place so more women and children could get together.

That sounded good to him. Of course, there were problems to iron out. There was no bathroom on this floor so our group would have to buy a bathroom and install it, and the front doors were kept locked so every mother would have to arrive exactly on time because of the custodian and what if a mother was late? And the board of directors wasn't going to meet again until the twenty-third but he'd talk to them.

Nancy said not to worry, that she'd take the problem of the

bathroom back to the group and we'd come up with something. She told him not to worry about the board of directors either; she'd talk to them herself and even bring some other women and a bunch of the children. The friendly young minister kept chuckling all through her offer and saying how it was really nice talking to her and to call him in three weeks.

The Presbyterian church board of directors met, but although our project was mentioned, there were more important things on the agenda.

The next board meeting was in six weeks and the friendly young minister would certainly do his best. Would Nancy come and talk about the bathroom? Nancy went and talked. The friendly young minister had been thinking this thing over. He was worried. Perhaps our group could draw up a proposal for the board of directors? Spell things out a little more clearly? How soon do you think you can get professional staffing? Volunteers *are so* unreliable—what if nobody shows up and the church is responsible for all those children? That is the kind of thing that is going to make the board very nervous.

Volunteers! We weren't volunteers. We were mothers! It was inconceivable that we wouldn't show up. The children needed us.

The Presbyterian church was still considering. We were still waiting. The record book was getting voluminous.

Kathy wrote that Phoebe liked to sit on her lap and be read to, alone. If anyone else came over to listen, Phoebe would get down and trot off without hearing the end of the story.

I kept writing about the fantasy games which I encouraged (meaning I didn't stop them). Sean's and Philip's major activity to begin with was to fight over who was going to be the daddy. Hitting and pinching and tears. It took a lot of convincing but we finally ended up with two daddies with Little Kelley and Bootsie as the two babies; Hagar was the grandfather and Whitney was the cat. Phoebe wanted to watch. It was a wonderful family.

Jinx kept reading the record book and it kept saying the same things about her daughter, Phoebe. She did things by herself. She did things with the mommy. She watched. No unhappiness. No change.

At one of our mothers' meetings, people started psyching Phoebe out and talking about the twins at home and sibling rivalry. I told about the game at the sandbox where they were all ducks and I went to buy them and there was all this quacking and waddling and Phoebe kept saying she was my special duck. And somebody said maybe Phoebe just liked being a special duck. She went around singing to herself. She was happy. And her mother wasn't worried, just very interested.

I *was* worried about Whitney, who was becoming the school punching bag. Every time Philip or Hagar or Sean felt frustrated, he or she would give Whitney a good punch. Then my daughter would do two things. She would release an ear-piercing scream followed by great sobs, and most important, she would never, never hit back.

A couple of women had read Ginott and, paraphrasing from his book would proclaim in ominous tones that "Whitney is not for hitting." But the obvious truth was, she was the perfect choice. Jinx said to buy her a punching bag, and Kelley and Nancy worried, too, and tried to toughen her up and at the same time be firmly in the middle before frustrations got out of hand.

The afternoon group was in good shape. The children took naps or rested listening to records or stories and then they went outside. Kay's daughter, Lisa, was their leader. This four-year-old organized everybody. She would put all of the children to bed and announce, "Now, I'm the mother and I'm damn nervous." Then, five minutes later, she would give them all an operation and then everyone would go to the movies and Lisa would be the movie.

It was hard to remember she was four. She was also taller and heavier than the other children. Constance was the biggest and strongest of the adults and she could pick Lisa up, but it wasn't easy. And we were trying not to treat her like a six-year-old and to be sure she got enough laptime and cuddling.

We decided we had to get the children out into the community even more, doing real things.

Jinx had a station wagon and took them to every playground in the city, and to Chinatown, across all the bridges, to the doll hospital, the Aquarium, the Indian museum, the Little Red Lighthouse, to all the zoos, to the fish market, the flower market, and the produce market.

I took them around the corner from my apartment where there was a nice little grocery with fruits and vegetables outside. I was disappointed that Whitney didn't know the difference between a grapefruit and a lemon and none of the children knew much about vegetables and they refused to believe that that green thing was an apple. Whitney was the diplomat who brought us all together. She said it was an apple, but not a real apple.

Kelley took them three blocks to the post office. Everyone helped mail a package to Little Kelley's grandmother. They got to see the man weigh the package, and to pay the money, and to see that package loaded on the mail truck. Kelley was going to have them all buy a penny stamp. But she forgot. Next time.

We also took the children on cultural trips, to the Museum of Natural History. They loved it. It had an elevator with a real man in it and a water fountain and you had to go on a bus to get there.

Nancy said she was perfectly happy except when she was outside with the kids. So she kept them in the apartment on Wednesday mornings. She would set up a bunch of dolls and doll clothes in one corner of the living room, some blocks in another, and they were free to build or nest all morning regardless of sex. Clay or gluing and painting things were on the dining room table, some puzzles and dress-up clothes in the bedroom, and children's books in the bathroom.

Kathy had been getting the children out in the community for a long time. She really wasn't nervous about traveling around with a pack of toddlers. She'd take them off on buses, on subways, or just on foot, trekking over to Riverside Park, over to the Cathedral of St. John the Divine, to the campus fountains, up to her office in the English Department, or to the fire station to look at the fire engine and pet the Dalmatian. Kathy would bop along to the supermarket to pick up something for snack or lunch, with Bootsie in her arms and everybody else running ahead and waiting at the curb. She said the children would be fine and they always were. But I worried and Nancy worried, and I don't know how many other people worried. Two of the children did get into the street the day Sean lost his shoe down the sewer. Kathy was trying to get hold of the kids and the shoe and not succeeding in doing either when she looked up and saw Hagar and Bootsie's daddy. He saw her and she told me later she knew she'd been caught being a bad mother. And Nancy told me he came home saying that Kathy was a dangerous woman, and they got into a big argument over it.

Buildings were still coming down all around us. We couldn't even get the children down 112th Street to Riverside Park anymore without all of us going into coughing fits from the flying debris.

Bank Street College of Education had decided to move up from Bank Street in Greenwich Village to become the seventeenth institution on Morningside Heights. Two more apartment houses were coming down. The Community Action Committee was out again stopping construction this time and organizing to keep the houses up and move families back into them. Proposals for low-income housing. Petitions with thousands of signatures rushed to the city fathers. Picket lines. Bank Street president calls the police. TV cameras. The concerned faculty shows up wearing little white badges. Meetings with the faculty where they keep saying this doesn't have anything to do with them and they can't seem to understand for a long time why we care. But they really are concerned and they vote against moving, but they are only the faculty and have no power.

Three women from our group kept telling me that Bank Street was a great place and now they might help us get a real professionally staffed daycare center. After all, they do *own* those buildings, you know.

My reply was neither unemotional nor genteel.

I had been out in the community again and everyone was asking me how the little school was coming along. I went back to the group and kept saying how we should put pressure on the church. Nobody did. We just waited. But not calmly.

There was that Thursday when Kathy had the children and Kelley brought Little Kelley and Sean up there late. Philip had his hands covered with orange paint and so did Hagar, and Sean got in line so Kathy could do him, and they were all going to make handprints on big sheets of white paper. The floor-level windows were open onto Kathy's fifth-floor balcony. A can of cockroach killer was sitting open on the table with the skull and crossbones shining in the sun. Kelley froze.

She talked to Kathy about something or other, made an excuse about Little Kelley's ear, and took her home. She wanted to take Sean, too, but couldn't think of a good reason.

The phones started ringing. Kelley wanted me to know what happened and what could we do about Kathy. Or, in other words, who was going to tell Kathy she was a rotten mother.

I was furious. Furious at Kelley. And I called Nancy right up to tell her. How could Kelley walk out of there with her daughter and leave Whitney and Hagar and Bootsie there to drink poison and walk off a fifth-story ledge? And what about Philip? My God, all she had to do was tell Kathy to put the stuff away and close the windows.

I knew I couldn't tell Kathy but somebody should.

Our survival depended on talking to each other, building trust, and sharing responsibility. But we had never had any training that would help us act in any of those ways. Being at home with little children softened us up, but we still had a lot of that good old American tradition of getting yours for you and your kid and getting out. In that big competition for best mother we edged ahead of Kathy. No one thought to offer her any help, such as suggesting she put in screens or window gates. We knew in our guts that there had been times in our own personal twenty-four-hour-a-day child-care operations—such as the time Jinx got the call from an irate neighbor when one of Jinx's twins was out on the windowsill; or the time I had poured an ounce of scalding water onto Whitney's chest; or the time Constance checked out of the grocery store and left Charlotte in her buggy in aisle four; but all those memories get stuffed back down inside. Not one of us wanted to be in competition. We hated it. But here we were again.

A couple of mothers made a few vague hints to Kathy. But she wasn't up to interpreting innuendoes. Ph.D. orals, that's all she could think of. Index cards typed with all the facts of Victorian literature were Scotch-taped to all her walls. Kathy memorized and crammed while she made Philip dinner, while she brushed her teeth, and while she took various concoctions to keep her stomach in one place and the contents from erupting.

So we had a meeting. Kelley Xeroxed a long list of "Safety Rules for the Home." (Great heavens! We were six people.) The rules were passed out at a meeting and everyone who had been phoned sat around saying how great they were and how we certainly would close all our windows, cover our wall sockets, never appear on the street with more than four children if we were by ourselves, lock all possibly harmful liquids in old suitcases, and on and on with more rules to cover possibilities in future generations.

Kathy read the rules for the first time, said they were a bunch of nonsense, an insult to the intelligence, that she resented rules being made at all, and that we should trust each other to take good care of the children.

Silence. Half of the women in the room were perspiring with embarrassment; the other half were sighing at this impossible woman. The subject was changed.

I said something about how *each woman had to be responsible for all the children, not just her own.* And Kelley said of course, we already were.

It didn't come up at the meeting, but everyone started saying to everyone else that *we had to start talking to each other.*

I'd like to say I sat down with Kathy and then with Kelley and had an honest conversation and then everything was fine. But I never did. No one did. Nancy told her husband all about it, the cockroach killer and open windows, and he said she was to keep the girls at home on Thursday mornings. And we went on with an absent-minded professor-to-be taking care of most of our children one morning a week. She was part of the community.

A celebration. Sean was three. Blanche and Sean lived in a room in somebody else's apartment, so she had the party in Riverside Park. A great idea. Everybody came. Blanche bought candy wheels for all the children. Sean got a little paint set, and some marbles, and some clay, and he couldn't stop smiling. It was a good day.

Somebody in our group managed to get Blanche a job at Teachers College so she didn't have that exhausting trek down-town. Kelley was working to get her into Hunter as a student. And she finally did with loans from the bank, but Blanche still couldn't make it to our meetings, and when she did, she would show up late and leave early, and she never offered us any news or advice or encouragement about our children.

Peggy came to all the meetings. She was worried about her son, Billy, who was hitting all the other children. Peggy said he was hitting the kids at his other nursery, the one he went to in the morning, and there had already been complaints about him there, but she didn't know what to do. Marilyn started telling her own son not to be bad like that bad Billy, and this upset half the group. The way Marilyn said it sounded natural, probably the same way her mother had warned her brother twenty years before. The women in our group were worried about Billy's being forever hung with that label, "bad kid." Peggy's friend told her what Marilyn said, and Peggy started calling around to see if it was true. She was angry. But we'd been through this sequence before and there was a change in the group. Four women, individually, told Peggy she was right to be mad, but that, of course, it wasn't going to do any good to tell them about it. She had to tell Marilyn. So Peggy finally got her nerve up. She phoned Marilyn and asked her not to call

Billy a bad boy. Marilyn said she wouldn't, and she didn't.

A few of the women who had had courses in psychology talked of the dangers of "role assignment" and one woman said that everyone should be careful because Marilyn obviously hadn't studied psychology and she might just say anything to your child.

But she never said anything much except that children should wash their hands and say please and thank you and stop hitting each other. And she wanted her son to grow up to be a good boy. And she took care of the children one afternoon every week and never missed. I remember her out on the campus, running across the grass with her arms outstretched, a big woman airplane with a brood of little baby airplanes running and falling down behind her.

Jesus, we really had to get to that church. Sean was three already and the institutions were out there chipping away at the neighborhood again. I had been organizing for a week. The Cathedral of St. John the Divine was trying to evict three elderly women from the building across the street from the church. The word came to the Community Action Committee office that the marshals were coming back Thursday and this time the church fathers were sending the police with them. So there we were at seven-thirty in the morning and by eleven it was all over. There was a lot of scurrying around and a lawyer appeared, who wanted to make it clear that it was *not* St. John the Divine who issued the eviction papers but Morningside House, a separate corporation of the Episcopal Archdiocese of New York. The lawyer also said that it was useless to fight. There were police already there, and more would come, if needed.

I had been leafleting the tourist buses, while the local canon jumped up and down on the cathedral steps, calling me a communist and an outside agitator, and saying he was glad to throw the old women out, that they had no legal right to remain.

I went upstairs to help the old women pack. Three old women. Flowered dresses. Ankles supported by tapes. Old-woman oxfords. Slow. Old.

I helped them pack their things in cardboard suitcases and old boxes. The women kept giving various possessions to strangers because it was easier to do that than to pack them. We carried the stuff into a neighbor's apartment, and one of the women said she'd packed her purse because she got confused and everybody was looking for it, but she couldn't remember which box.

And I went home and looked at the wall and wished the children weren't coming in the morning. I didn't want to see anyone.

Sunday there were community church services on the cathedral steps. Half the women in our group came. People brought children, bread, wine, sad feelings. Passed them around.

Everybody wanted to know how the little school was coming along. Did we have a place yet? Mary was there from 110th Street with her son David in his stroller and her daughter Melorra running around. She had a lot of professional credentials in daycare and other areas, and said to use her name and all her credentials on any papers or proposals or bureaucratic forms if they would help. Sharing the credentials. But we didn't get a chance.

The Presbyterian church turned us down. They gave our project a great deal of thought, and while it was terribly worthy and a good undertaking and they certainly wished us luck, the church fathers felt that what the community really needed was a program for Columbia freshmen.

Depression. Nancy had had enough. She went back into her Wednesday mornings, set up new areas all over her house, put some music on the record player just for herself, and decided to go off with Blanche on Saturdays because Blanche was her friend and because she didn't trust her on the subways and buses with the children.

We still needed space. A place for the children out in the community that would be theirs, where they could be with each other every day and be taken care of: a sanctuary.

We had been together for months because we needed each other. We didn't have much to put on a proposal. We hadn't developed a theory of education or attached ourselves to one or elected a president, or a board of directors, or any committees, or raised any money. We spent all our time wandering around the neighborhood trying to hold onto our anxieties and share our children.

Dear Gentlemen of Columbia and affiliates in the Morningside Heights Institutional Complex:

We are thirteen families who are sharing the care of our children six days a week from nine in the morning to five in the evening. We all live in the neighborhood, mostly in apartments you own. We use a different apartment every morning as a place to take care of the children and we use a basement (which you also own) during the afternoons.

It has been a rough year largely because of these makeshift arrangements. And because we have had to say no to many women and children who wanted to join the group because our apartments are too small and the playroom is too small for any more people.

It was also a difficult year because all the children cried at first. I don't know what else to say. They're all healthy. Little Kelley still has her bad ear. But doctors have changed their theories on tonsils. Now they leave them in. You will be glad to know that Sean is three at last. He is talking very well, and crying and fighting and he plays with Bootsie a lot. He hugs and kisses her when she falls down. He can do twenty-four-piece puzzles and knows the days of the week, but is still having trouble naming his colors.

If you could see your way clear to share some of your excess property that is currently unused and/or some of your excess money that is currently unused with the women and children of the neighborhood, please contact Ms. Harlow at . . .

But you couldn't put that kind of thing on a proposal. This was serious business.

With that thought in mind, I took over the getting-space-in-the-neighborhood, getting-legal-in-the-city, getting-money-to-get-all-those-things-that-you-have-to-pay-for-to-get-legal project. I called up Kelley and the two of us went rushing off into institutional channels.

3. Institutional Complex

If you go rushing off into institutional channels you will have to give up any idea of talking directly to people, using your own experience, being responsible for your own children, staying close, or sharing.

We went rushing off to the institutions because they were there. And because there were women and children who needed the help the institutions could give us. And because we couldn't go traipsing around from apartment to apartment every morning with seven children and spend our afternoons down in a basement with twelve children. It was January.

The six months of negotiations with the Presbyterian church were down the drain. The church fathers had cited their obligations to Columbia University.

The university. It had unused rooms, apartments, storefronts, buildings, and a significant control over the unused space of the other neighborhood institutions. And $10 million from the Ford Foundation to set up an Urban Center and do good work in the community.

So it was just a matter of getting together with some of that money and some of that space.

There we were, Kelley and Nora, two anti-institutional people desperate to go running off into the proper institutional channels. But it wasn't that simple.

There were rules.

And those rules got us in deeper. Farther from ourselves, farther from the children, and certainly farther from any sense of sharing or community.

Not only did we have to find out the hierarchical workings and bureaucratic intricacies of the university, we even had to find out what *we* were supposed to be. We knew what we were before we had decided to interact with these institutions. Simple: we were thirteen adults who shared the care of their eighteen babies from nine to five from Monday through Saturday every week of the year. In our minds we already were a functioning daycare group. That was a nice idea. But, of course, that's not the point of an official daycare center.

The city fathers had defined a daycare institution very carefully and had written rules governing the legal care of children outside their own homes. The rules were all in a little white book titled:

The City of New York–Department of Health
Bureau of Child Health
Division of Day Care, Day Camps, and Institutions
125 Worth Street
New York, N.Y., 10013

Kelley managed to get a copy. Kelley and I pored over the rules and with eight years of college training between us we did a pretty fair translation of most of them. We had braced ourselves, but not enough. After about an hour of translating a lot of convoluted officialese beginning with "No person shall . . ." and "Every person must . . ." with a lot of "pursuant to . . ." and "footcandles per . . ." and "prophylaxis for . . ." my adrenaline was jumping around my body and then there it was, Rule No. 45.1, subsection (i), "In regard to urinals . . ." which pointed out the inconsistencies within the code itself between S.C. 198, S.C. 200 Reg. 14(b), S.C. 203 Reg. 11, and of course, C26-1279.0. It seems one code provision required "at least one-fourth of the required number of fixtures to be water closets," another did not mention urinals, yet another provided that urinals could be substituted for toilets, but required that the number of water closets could not be reduced below two-thirds the required number, and another provision stated flatly that the code required "schools to provide water closets [*sic*] for at least one-fourth of the required number of fixtures," while at the same time providing that "when urinals are substituted for toilets the number of toilets shall not be reduced below two-thirds the required number." And then there was a discussion of the error in the use of the term "water closet," that, indeed, "urinal . . . represents the true intention of the law." And then the capper, in black and white and official: "Urinals are not required."

I couldn't stand it. These people are crazy. They're obsessive compulsive paranoid old men who've never taken care of a child in their lives. They think they are sane because they are very quiet and controlled and have managed to persuade a lot of other people to participate in their delusions.

They had a control for every possible adult action. The rules were more than absurd or funny or authoritarian or cold. The rule writers knew mankind. They knew greed and evil. Most of all they knew their duty. Their little book was based on the premise that grown-up people must be prevented from carrying out their basic desire to herd masses of their offspring into tiny wet basements, keep them in the dark, with no air, sweep dirt into their faces, and feed them warm sour milk, while coughing up blood into a dirty handkerchief with one hand and raking in a tidy American profit with the other. The way they were going to prevent this was to write rules saying you couldn't, plus a lot of other rules which specified exactly how small the room could be, how dark you could keep it, and how warm the milk could be, plus specification after specification about the physical surroundings. They also demanded that anyone having anything to do with children, besides the ones they gave physical birth to, have several institutional certificates, a college education, and, of course, the city fathers' own impersonal stamp of approval.

The staff requirements reeked of the assumption that it was dangerous for noninstitutional women or men to supervise children, more dangerous for uneducated people to be with children, and extremely dangerous for a poor and uneducated woman to care for children—even her own.

The rules were very hostile.

There were more and more of them. "The person holding himself out as conducting a day care service" must also pledge himself to maintain a sterile surrounding for the children with no rugs, or drapes, or pillows, or overstuffed chairs that might get dirty.

The little white book was to be displayed prominently in all daycare centers in case anyone forgot the rules. That was another rule.

After three hours I was giddy with emotion, doing a stand-up comic routine on each new rule. If I could keep laughing maybe I wouldn't feel so threatened. Kelley and I were just sitting there laughing and I was clutching her arm: "This *is* all crazy—crazy and wrong."

"Yes." Kelley was steady, practical. She was applying to law school. She didn't like the rules, but they were there and had to be coped with. Kelley had receded into herself, adopted her composed face, and pressed her efficiency button.

I walked home depressed and anxious.

Nancy and I had made loud declarations from the very beginning that no child should be in an institution and no adult either and every woman absolutely agreed, but though we damned every bureaucratic, officialese, institutional dictum that controlled and dehumanized our lives, we were still hanging on. We were so used to it.

Institutions were what we knew.

Once I asked Jinx why she was in the group. She thought it out carefully. It was right for her because she wanted Phoebe in a group in the neighborhood and she wanted her to play with children from different backgrounds and she (Jinx) wanted to be in it. She said she loved taking care of the children and she was putting Phoebe in a good private school when she was four.

Kathy kept saying we were so middle class and that our setup was O.K. for us, personally great for her—she'd never get through her Ph.D. without it—but what she wanted was a daycare center that would serve poor women who really had a need.

Constance and Demi and Peggy and even Nancy had their children in regular nurseries for half a day. To get them ready for kindergarten and real school.

Nancy complained that she had to pay twice as much tuition as everyone else because it was a Columbia nursery school and she was a neighborhood person, but she was lucky to get Hagar in at all and that was only because they had decided to integrate. With Hagar in, Bootsie was almost assured of a place when she was old enough. The teachers were progressive, they didn't push, and they even let the parents come in occasionally and watch the children through a two-way mirror.

Constance loved Edmund's nursery teacher. She put him in when he was three and it was Constance's first bit of freedom. The nursery was a parent cooperative for Columbia faculty only. Constance was continually puzzled by some of the mothers. They just sat around. They couldn't even get the clay out in the morning until the teacher told them. These women were astounded that our group was in existence and firmly convinced that they couldn't take care of a group of children all on their own as Constance did, since their degrees weren't in early education.

The women in our group were all horrified.

Constance was the most horrified and also the most convinced that our group wasn't real since we didn't have a person designated "teacher."

There were more complaints about other nurseries—large fees, short hours, lots of holidays, waiting lists, all of the children from the same kind of family and just alike. But the competition to get in was intense. Constance was getting her four-year-old son ready for a series of interviews at private schools.

Jane and Marilyn were saving their money and putting off nursery at least until the children were four. Maybe they could even wait until they were five and get them in a public school program. And the public schools—one could complain forever about them.

It was unnerving. Everyone talked about how good it was to have the group and share the children and talk to each other about the children, to use our own experience, to stay close to the children, and how easy it was, and how marvelous for them personally and how they loved all the children and how happy the children were and at the same time they were putting their children in real schools with real teachers and real administrators as soon as possible and at a great personal sacrifice.

Maybe when they found out how far we were from being a real child institution like in the rules they would all just leave.

Kelley and I would stay. We were solid. And Blanche would stay—she had no other place to go. And Constance and Demi and Nancy each still had a younger child who wouldn't be accepted anywhere else.

Two days later Nancy called me up. She had been reading the little white book.

She had worked herself up into a real fear of authority. Those rules were demoralizing. We could never fulfill all those stipulations. Besides, we'd probably never get a chance because nearly the first rule said that since she had six unrelated children in her apartment on Wednesday mornings the city fathers could send the police to arrest her. I told her the police would probably never arrest her or even come to her apartment and they would probably never arrest any of us and we both knew that was true. But Nancy was still upset. The fact remained that they had written this rule saying she was breaking the law. Nancy didn't like the whole idea and she wasn't completely certain she should stay in the group.

She told all the women at the meeting and they all looked at Kelley and me and I looked at the floor and said yes, taking care of our children was against the law, unless we took care of less than six children or we took care of them for less than five hours a week, or for less than one month a year. Anything more than that and we were viewed by the city fathers as running an illegal daycare service and they had all these rules. And it wouldn't even help us if we did less. The city fathers had rules for that, too. Then we came under their Family Day Care regulations. And we were still illegal. Sharing children was completely against their code.

Jinx and Blanche and Marilyn and Jane and Constance and Demi and Peggy refused to believe we were really illegal. They believed the rule was there but they just couldn't concentrate on it. I mean, no policeman was going to come and arrest them. That was absurd. They weren't starting a daycare center, anyway. That was Kelley and Nancy and I. They were simply taking care of children, that's all. This daycare business was a whole different thing.

Constance and Demi were too busy with so many different schools and nursery situations for their children and babysitting pools and being in school themselves to worry about city officials. They both said they were in favor of daycare. They didn't need it themselves, but there were so many women who did. Anyway they were for it.

We talked on about the children. Kelley Marie, as Little Kelley insisted on calling herself now, was afraid of subway grilles and would start shrieking if she felt she was getting too near one. Hagar thought she was the bravest person alive because she tiptoed across one. Billy was still hitting the other children. Kelley said Billy was very bright and very sensitive. He could add and subtract and read a little bit. He had an unbelievable amount of concentration but sometimes social situations got way out of his control. It helped sometimes if the grownup made him sit on a chair by himself for a minute till he could get himself back under control. Sometimes just holding him still—like a big hug, but firm—helped. It was even better if you could get there before he got that far and help him work it out with the children before it got to hitting. Sean was resisting being put on the toilet by force but Blanche had said it was a must. Actually he wasn't resisting too much. He knew he wasn't supposed to go in his pants and he'd even been giggling when Nancy picked him up from his game this morning and made him sit on the toilet. He was going to get over this business fast. We were all tired of wet pants. And Bootsie was better than anyone else on the trapeze. Bootsie! The great puzzle was how she even managed to get her two-year-old self up there. I saw her do it, but I still couldn't understand it.

No one mentioned the city or its rules or its police anymore.

Nancy asked me to please come and talk to her friend Mary on 110th Street with all the credentials.

Mary had a Ph.D., was a psychologist. She treated patients, taught at Brooklyn College, had taught kindergarten for several years in the public schools, and had been very much involved with a community daycare group in Newark, New Jersey.

We sat in Mary's kitchen while she made tea for us with baby David on her hip. Her three-year-old daughter was downstairs at the babysitter's. Whitney, Hagar, Bootsie, and the gang were at Jinx's apartment, making butter by shaking up cream in a mayonnaise jar with a marble in it.

Kelley was in her apartment sorting out the rules into categories —those that were totally stupid, those that the officials might hassle us on, the two or three that we would fulfill anyway out of common sense, plus those that were worth considering if we had the resources.

Mary said she wasn't there during the formation of the Newark daycare project and she hadn't read the rules but she didn't think they were all that bad.

But that was the whole point: I didn't want to fight the city fathers about any rules. And I certainly didn't want to prove to them that I was fit to take care of children or that my friends were —especially by fulfilling all their rules that I felt were unfit.

Silence.

Mary said the Newark project grew right out of the community. It started with a small group in a church basement and grew into a giant daycare complex in lots of church basements and storefronts with four thousand children and $2.5 million in government funds.

Mary said we had to be careful. Funding could ruin us. The people in Newark had been dedicated, hard workers. Then there was $2.5 million and less hard work. There was a lot of competition for that money and some dedicated community people dropped out and some were forced out. Then there was the reality of the fund's being withdrawn or cut and someone had to plead with the authorities for money and some salaries had to be cut and some people had to be laid off. The desperation of the whole process changed the best people and mostly the best people didn't even notice.

I knew Mary meant well. But Nancy and Kelley and I with $2.5 million and four thousand kids? Impossible. I couldn't even work up a fantasy about it. So I had a fantasy about $80,000 and forty or fifty kids instead. I would run the center, of course. I'd be down at City Hall screaming and yelling every other day and I'd whip those people into shape and I'd have a salary of $10,000 or maybe $15,000. . . . No, all that screaming and yelling and defending the group and raising more funds and I'd have to go up to Albany a lot—that was worth $22,500, I thought, wiping the drool off my chin. Of course, Kelley might want the job, but she was leaving in June when her husband graduated. I would have to consider the fact that I didn't *want* to direct a daycare center, but then I wasn't going to get an opportunity like this every day and the group wasn't going to find a person with my dedication growing on a bush.

Oh, shut up, Nora.

Nancy was asking for reassurance from Mary that we weren't hurting the children. Mary wasn't certain.

Nancy and Mary and I had read many baby books and many baby authorities and all the books and all the authorities were firm on one point. Children needed a stable environment. One person. A woman. A mother. And then later, one woman, the nursery teacher who had had a minimum of 150 clock hours of observation and supervised practice with children and who would arrange for the children to go through the same routines every day until they were secure.

I said the changes in our children were obvious. They were gaining a sense of themselves and a definite security in the adult world. They had lots of time to form strong friendships with each other. We spent most of every parents' meeting talking about how happy they all were.

Nancy said that maybe happiness wasn't enough. And they might not be as happy as they could be. Sometimes there wasn't much follow-through. She was still suspicious of what some of the other women were doing with the children. And there were children who needed stability, like Sean. He had now decided he wouldn't go anywhere with anybody and the last time Nancy had worked he had refused to go across the street to the playroom when the morning was over and he bit Nancy when she was trying to put his shoes on.

Besides, to be legal we had to get the approval of an agency person in charge of daycare and there just wasn't an agency person in the world who wasn't going to shrink with horror at the idea of all those untrained people with those little babies. Nancy and Mary agreed that the children who were in our group all day must be having it rough—like Sean (and Whitney).

There wasn't much I could say except I didn't think so. I was outnumbered by Nancy and Mary and all the books and all the experts.

Anyway, Mary came up with a very appealing idea. She said the one really good thing she saw at the Newark center was the community participation and she remembered an elderly man who used to come in every day and play with the children and the children were crazy about him.

Maybe we could cut through all the institutional crap and hire a woman—maybe an older woman from the neighborhood. Or a man. A person who would not be responsible for organizing the center or running it or doing any of the hard work, just someone who had a natural ability with children who would come in every day and be there with her comfortable lap and some soft words. Someone who would remember where Bootsie's extra pants were, and to remind Sean to go to the bathroom and that Kathy was picking up Philip at twelve instead of one and that Kelley Marie should stay in again today because of her cold.

Nancy and I sighed. Not just for the children. We wanted that woman for us, too.

Mary spoke of Marianna, her babysitter, as that kind of person. I had a vision of my godmother, Dorothy. Dorothy took care of her three boys and she took care of me during the week while my mother worked in the factory and my father was off fighting the war. Dorothy would hide me under the towel in her ironing basket and everybody hunted for me or she would move the dishes and put little Russell up in the cabinet or on top of the refrigerator or unmake the bed and put us both where the pillows were.

I knew that my mother would never have left me with any old

babysitter off the street and neither my mother nor Dorothy would have put me or any of their children in an institution. Mother could leave me with Dorothy because Dorothy knew that I was an important child.

A babysitter might not really know that in her guts. And an institution couldn't ever know that any child was important. Even the best teachers couldn't know a child was important when their commitment to that child was for a few months, when their commitment to that neighborhood didn't exist, when even their teaching-nurturing commitments were strictly controlled by administrators, syllabuses, federal, state, city rules and money, by unions, and even by the training institutions they had already passed through.

Mary said for the hundredth time that morning that we must use our own experience. That was the most important thing to remember. Then she loaded us both up with piles of literature on how to start a daycare center, how to teach in a daycare center, how to buy materials for a daycare center, how to . . .

We said maybe when we had a place set up she would like her daughter, Melorra, in the group, and she said maybe sometime but not all day and not for a while because she had this arrangement with Marianna.

That was a grand idea, hiring a person like Dorothy, or Marianna, or that man in Newark. And it fitted in so well with our continuing illusion that we could develop some kind of brand-new nurturing educational community for our children right in the neighborhood run by all the people in it on completely humanistic lines. And furthermore, we were going to launch this anti-institutional, unstructured, nonhierarchical, noncapitalistic venture with the complete support of all the existing overstructured, hierarchical, capitalistic institutions and with their money and without bullshitting a lot on proposals. We told Kelley all about our visit with Mary in minute detail. After listening very carefully, Kelley made up the proposed budget. It was a very progressive document.

There were reasonable salaries for two group teachers who would be certified and stamped, and for four teacher-aides who would be paid half as much as the real teachers, but who would be encouraged to lift themselves up by their own bootstraps and go to school and get stamped and certified also.

There was a salary for a cook and there were funds for social services, psychological services, medical services, utilities, housekeeping, food, renovations, annual repair, expendable materials, telephone, office supplies, special programs (trips, etc.), and, of course, social security, insurance, and auditing.

That was all we needed to care for thirty-five children and it would cost only $57,500 the first year and less after that. It was so cheap compared to city budgets because Columbia would provide the space free of charge and because the parents and all kinds of neighborhood people would contribute services free of charge and because we were so clever with the money and so honest.

Kay heard about a militant black woman who had set up a day-care center in the next neighborhood down and we went off to talk to her.

Dorothy Pittman certainly had no fear of authority. She said to do it and dare them to close us. It was harder for the city to close a place that was open than a place that was trying to open. It had taken her less than two weeks to start her center. She and her sister rented a dilapidated storefront in the neighborhood, which was full of dilapidated empty storefronts and had already been designated a poverty area, knocked on doors to find children of working women, charged them $12 a week, and that's all there was to it.

She said we should keep it in the neighborhood and keep the parents a part of it—because it was good and because a couple of people could never do it all alone. She said to forget the rulebook. The rules weren't written with our needs in mind. In fact, they didn't have anything to do with us at all.

The city officials had found her group eventually and came storming down on their storefront, looked around the place for about ten minutes, gave everybody twenty minutes to vacate, and said they were padlocking the place.

Dorothy just told them no. Not unless they arrested every person there and all the children and dragged them out.

She said she was hoping they would get arrested because the group was desperate for funds and really needed the publicity. But no arrests and no padlocks. Dorothy talked to them about the children and the neighborhood and their problems and they talked to her about the bathroom and how it was impossible. And she said it was the city's job to see that the bathroom *was* possible and it was not their job to go around closing down neighborhood daycare centers.

I wished Nancy had been there. I told the group about Dorothy but all they seemed to understand was that Kay and I were impressed.

Our situations weren't exactly similar. Morningside Heights wasn't a designated poverty area. There were no storefronts for rent. Nobody in our group wanted to direct a daycare center but everybody wanted to be with the children and we didn't want to charge each other money for that.

Kelley called another meeting, this time with lots of institutional people from the neighborhood. There was a dean's wife, who seemed to have no name of her own, but was forever being referred to as Dean So-and-So's wife. She had contacts with forty-three different organizations who could help us in some way or give us advice. And there was a man from Bank Street who organized committees on daycare and had had seminars and weekend conferences and there were interminable discussions about the current battles to change certain regulations, and the ins and outs of city bureaucracy, and whom to talk to in the city bureaus and whom not to talk to in the city bureaus. There was talk of funding or mainly lack of funding and of the five centers that had closed that week from lack of money and of the new kinds of equipment that were just coming out on the market.

A student from S.D.S. said he couldn't take any more of this stuff and he left.

Two women were there who had worked in the freedom schools in the South. They had come north to take courses at Teachers College on 120th Street, and they didn't say anything. Kelley finally asked them what they did about equipment. They both said the same thing. Equipment wasn't a problem. People brought stuff in and built things and they just used whatever was around. The problem was getting the space. Get the space, take the children in, and that's all you need.

Those were sweet words. I told my husband I was getting tired of going to meetings to talk about starting a daycare center, I just wanted to do it. He couldn't understand why we were meeting with all those people. Hadn't we (I) learned anything at all from the year of '68 at Columbia or from the tenant fight or from the Community Action Committee or from the evictions?

Kelley went home and called up forty-three different organizations, all of which said their group never handled that kind of thing but they could refer her to three other organizations that did, or that the person who handled that sort of thing was out or that starting a daycare center was an interesting idea and they would get back to her on it.

Then Kelley called a meeting of all the interested parents in the group to try to get this thing more organized.

What can I say about that meeting? It was an epic.

We started off slowly by trying to think of a name for ourselves. We couldn't go around forever calling ourselves a group of Morningside Heights mothers. The People's School. Two people thought that maybe that sounded too Chinese or like communists. Four others said, "Yeah!" with big grins on their faces. Then someone suggested the Children's Free School. And that was it. Free meant it was free. Nobody had to pay money. Free meant the children would be free to grow at their own pace and follow their own interests. Free meant that the mothers would be free from incessant child care. Free meant that no official we had never seen before and would never see again would be allowed to come in one day with a book of rules and tell us what to do. The grownups and children would run the school. Self-determination. Community control.

Then. We discussed very seriously two simultaneous plans of action. One, we would form our own board of directors, get ourselves incorporated and tax-exempt, follow every rule in all the books, get a lawyer and an accountant, and press for funds from Columbia's Urban Center's Ford Foundation millions. Two, we would all legally adopt all of each other's children so that none of the city fathers or the police or any other public official would ever be able to touch us.

Most people in the group thought we should follow through on both plans immediately. Then we had a tawdry discussion about who we would let in and who we would keep out of the Children's Free School when we got official.

Everyone agreed that acceptance should be on the basis of need. Unfortunately that idea was permanently allied to the old white Christian missionary concept of uplifting poor unfortunates and also mixed in with the idea that only poor, wretched, single, or unfit mothers needed daycare because all the others could bloody well stay home with their children or use their husbands' money to hire babysitters.

Kay and Jane and Constance immediately announced that they didn't really need daycare, which was the same as saying that they were not poor or wretched and that they were certainly capable of taking care of their own children and doing it very well. Which left us trying to figure out who had the most need—a mother who was voluntarily poor because she was finishing her schooling or a mother who was hard-core poor because she was born that way. From that we went on to the child locked away in an apartment with grandmother all day vs. the child who was sent to one private nursery in the morning, picked up and lunched by a babysitter, and delivered to another private nursery in the afternoon, then picked up by another babysitter and kept till 6 P.M. And what about a woman who just wanted her child to have friends and wanted some time by herself to think about what she would do if she ever had any time to herself?

Somebody interrupted to say we would have to be careful because there were lots of women who felt so desperate they would lie their heads off just to get in and somebody else said that if they felt that desperate, why didn't we just let them in?

A revolutionary idea: the woman herself could determine if she had a need. If she said she or her child had a need they had a need and they were in. The people could choose the school instead of the school choosing the people. There was no reason to have any waiting lists anywhere or any screening committees. When ten to fifty families were listed, they could just get together and start another school.

There was an impatient voice of reason—male—saying we couldn't possibly let everybody in, that was ridiculous, and if we were really honest we'd have to say that a woman on welfare with five or six children certainly had more right to be in a daycare center than anybody in this room. Obviously at some point we would have to set up a screening committee to go over the applications but we didn't even have a school yet, so we didn't have to talk about all that now.

I agreed. What we should talk about was *his* working with our children. "You know, it would be very good for the children, it would make them very happy if you could come and play with them sometimes." He laughed. Todd had laughed too, when Kelley had first asked him to come and play with the children. Lester had laughed when I asked him. I couldn't figure out what was so damn funny. And I was getting dark looks from some of the women. There wasn't going to be any talk about the babies tonight.

The talk had to be serious because the men were there. They were there tonight because they were interested in their children and because we were talking money and real estate, which was serious.

It was Todd who wanted to set up a board of directors. Nearly everyone laughed, but then we started to choose ~~men~~ people for the board. Kelley and I insisted that if we had a board, every adult in the group should be on it.

Then my husband, Lester, announced that he would definitely not be on the board of directors. In fact, he had no intention of having anything to do with any group that was doing business with the Ford Foundation.

I was stunned. What did he think he was doing? Lester hadn't spent one minute taking care of any of the children with us. Now he was on his political high horse, keeping himself pure, causing dissension by making pronouncements about "any group" that did this or that. He didn't even look my way. It seemed not to cross his mind that "any group" was his wife and daughter. I was so angry my face was bright hot. I was fervently praying it hadn't turned red because I was pretending to the group that nothing had happened.

The discussion on the floor continued. Three people asked, "What's wrong with the Ford Foundation?" Two more explained that it wasn't the Ford Foundation anyway. It was the university. And all that money was just across the street but if we wanted any of it we would have to get over there fast because $8 million was gone already and rather mysteriously, according to articles in the Columbia *Spectator*, and there had been talk of an investigation and the last $2 million might disappear any day now. The Ford money was just to get started.

We were going to use city tax money to run the center. That was ours, anyway. Of course, in order to get to use any of our money there were these rules we had to follow. First of all we would get so much a head for each poor child. But only if we managed to meet our quota of poor children, which was something like 80 percent. We also had to arrange a suitable sliding scale of payments, examine each family's personal financial situation, to make sure nobody who could afford to pay was getting any of that money.

Silence. In effect, eight people were all saying that we did want to get to poor people who really had a need.

I said I would not paint white picket fences in Harlem. Making people prove that they were the poorest citizens in the community and that they were also the least able to take care of their own children was a despicable activity. What did people think they were doing when they made other people prove that? It was degrading, demoralizing, and made me want to vomit. What a rotten way to join a group! Of course the poor weren't supposed to join. That was the whole point.

Constance's husband said they weren't going to give you money to take care of your own children.

Lester said he agreed with me. I smiled. O.K., he was on my side again. I hoped he would stay there.

Kelley recited the budget.

Jane's husband, a lawyer, wanted to know why there was no allotment for rent in the budget and where was the center going to be? Someone said Columbia was going to give us some space for free, which made him smile. "Why should they do that?"

Lester said if they didn't we should just liberate some Columbia space and take the children in. I wished he would at least get to know these people better before he hit them with such statements.

Jane's husband said that was private property. Columbia owned it and we had no right to it.

Then I was yelling, how much could you own? This wasn't a neighborhood. This was a plantation.

Todd wanted to know who was going to be on the board of directors so we could get this finalized.

Jane's husband said to leave his name off for a while. He'd see how things went.

Lester said again he would definitely not have his name added to the board.

By now, I was furious, but I said nothing. I couldn't oppose my husband in public. I didn't even want to. I busied myself doing the wifely thing, pretending I didn't notice, pretending that that particular man's opinions didn't affect me.

Kelley noticed, though. She said that maybe we shouldn't have a board of directors.

Todd said nobody was going to do business with you if you didn't have a board of directors. I mumbled to Kelley that I didn't want to *do business*. Todd tried to get somebody to be president, vice-president, and secretary. All the men talked.

Kelley was silent.

I was silent.

After a while people started putting on their coats. Kelley reminded us that the children had to be at her apartment by nine-thirty tomorrow because she and Jinx were taking them to the Aquarium.

I don't know what Kelley and Todd talked about after we left, but all the way home I was having fantasies, fantasies that were building in the breadth and scope of their violence. I pictured myself slugging Lester, making him bleed, lose teeth, say he was sorry. The fantasies were particularly bloody being locked up in a female body that had been instructed to be a lady, if nothing else. This lady had never slugged anybody, would never slug anybody, but she could talk. So as soon as we entered our living room I let Lester have it. How *dare* he destroy what I'd been working so hard for? What was the idea of spending all that time talking about the Ford funds as tainted money? What did he mean he wasn't going to have anything to do with the group? How could he be such a bastard?

I had spent months trying to hold this whole thing together. I needed these people. Whitney needed them. Lester could afford to be idealistic and politically correct because he didn't have to stay alone in the apartment with his daughter day after day or even spend all day Thursday taking care of all the children. He didn't need a daycare center. If the neighborhood never got a daycare center together it wouldn't ruin his life—just Whitney's and mine.

Lester said he was sorry. He wasn't sorry he said those things. He was only sorry I got upset. He started to question my politics. (He didn't say it in so many words but I got the message: "Give a woman a baby and her politics go all to hell.") What he said was that I shouldn't play so innocent. I knew what the Ford Foundation was all about. I knew the kind of money the Ford Motor Company made and that there were all those people on the factory line and all those secretaries processing orders and all those people cleaning up the place making nominal sums and the profits were so huge that the bosses set up a foundation as a tax dodge so they could still control that money and parcel it out as charity to a few approved people and get all kinds of thanks and praise and at the same time keep their hierarchy totally intact and keep all these people below them dependent and grateful and asking daddy for a handout.

Silence.

He was absolutely right. But he was still a bastard.

And Kelley had already mailed her letters to the president of Columbia and the president of the Urban Center. There was an appointment with somebody in the Urban Center office scheduled for Wednesday. And I was going with Kelley and Lisa's daddy to meet this person.

4. Village Child Care vs. the Institutional Complex

The Urban Center office was different. There were black secretaries everywhere, which was unusual for a university office in 1969. I immediately thought of that black man Columbia hired to throw out all the black and Puerto Rican families as part of the institution's campaign to clean up the neighborhood. To make the neighborhood safe for people. But that thought didn't make any sense, I told myself, doubtless another bit of my hopeless paranoia setting in—block it out—and besides, this wasn't even a university office. This was the Urban Center. The Ford Foundation.

The administrator to whom we had been referred was still out to lunch. We waited. We were tense. Kelley had assured us this meeting would be easy. She was worried that our ideas for child care might be too revolutionary for the establishment, but she felt that with patience we could win them over. And we did have a program going, a successful program; that was an important factor. We had a budget that was certainly not a ripoff of anybody's money. That should be impressive. The Urban Center had been heavily criticized in the community, but that was because they were from outside the neighborhood and because there was no way for the people to get to them. We just had to open the channels of communication.

Don was a bit more doubtful. He was a community contact person for the Board of Education and used to dealing with institutional personnel.

Finally the administrator came rushing in, apologized for being late, and all three of us said that was perfectly all right. She was black, petite, well coiffed, well dressed, and attractive. Personable. She was a nice person, you could tell that in one minute. She was understanding. Nobody had to convince her about the need for daycare. She had a son. He was in a private school now.

Kelley and I talked about the nice things we were doing with the children, and explained how well it worked to have lots of people with the children. We spoke of our hopes for the future and explained how the city figure was $3,000 per child per year and that with the community included in the program that could be cut to less than $2,000, and after the first year to less than $1,500 *and* the actual benefits to the children would be even greater than with the larger budget. She was very patient. Don asked her what she thought of the budget. She said she had read it and that she was glad we had come to see her first and that she certainly wanted to help us. Don made another indirect reference to money.

The administrator looked away and said it was unfortunate that the Urban Center was so often thought of as a funding agent. She seemed truly unhappy.

I asked what the Urban Center did do.

The Urban Center's job was to "make the resources of Columbia University available to the community." "Resources" did not mean money or space or the library or the teaching staff or . . .

I asked her what "resources" did mean.

No real answer. The office would like to do whatever they could to help us. There were intimations that this was a big favor that the administrator was undertaking personally. After all, we were told, the office considered Harlem the community.

Kelley and I both said that one of the group's intentions was to locate near Harlem because we felt strongly that our group should include families from both communities. She ignored that remark and somehow I felt guilty about having made it.

The administrator was becoming more a friend and less a person who was going to sign a check. In her professional opinion, and she knew a great deal about the ins and outs of daycare programs, she didn't think we were ready to accept money or space. This made me nervous. Was there something wrong with the proposal? No answer. She understood us and felt we could probably even handle it, but other, less sympathetic officials might not be understanding. She was being very gentle with us and very kind, which made the air in the room so thick I couldn't keep from coughing. Kelley's face was a blank and she seemed to be at a great distance from me. Don was shuffling some papers on his lap.

Did we understand about incorporation? We would have to get incorporated before we approached anybody for funding. Who could a funding body even give the money to? It wouldn't be legal. A low chuckle. We must also elect a president, a vice-president, and a treasurer, and get a board of directors.

Kelley said that the parents would be the board of directors.

The administrator replied that the formation of the board was very important. Get a lawyer and a doctor on the board and look for people with money and, more important, with connections. Substantial citizens. Our kind of group would need these kinds of people. Funding was always a problem for any group. Especially the second, third, or fourth year. And if you have a few people who can get to the right people in the right places, make some phone calls, mention our group at some private dinner parties . . . She gave us a confidential smile. This little tidbit was not for quotation, but just among friends, we all knew how the world worked.

Somehow we just couldn't smile back. What about parents on the board?

She thought that one-third of the board members could be parents—the laws were being liberalized.

Could the lawyers and substantial people be parents also?

We had lost her. Frowns. No response.

Don brought us all back to the point of our visit once again and tried to get her to be concrete about what kind of commitment the Urban Center could make to us.

But she didn't want to talk about commitment in specific ways. I mean, the office *was* committed to the community, that's why she was talking to us right at that moment. She wanted to help us. For one thing, the city was going to be a difficult obstacle. The Urban Center too had had trouble with the city. There was no use even approaching the city people until we had familiarized ourselves with the daycare rules. The first thing we had to do was get a copy of the book of rules for Day Care, Day Camps, and Institutions.

Kelley and I both said we had a copy.

The administrator recovered from her surprise. Well, of course, it wasn't enough just to read it. Unfortunately, and we might not like this, but we should memorize this book. We should know those rules backward and forward and inside out. When we had our first meeting with the Bureau of Child Welfare people, we should know their regulations better than they did. She was about to launch into several other helpful ideas when Kelley asked a question.

Why couldn't the Urban Center fund us, since we were a bona fide community group and the money was for the community?

Pause. Calm. Then the administrator told a lie. She said the office never gave financial assistance to daycare programs.

Kelley said the Urban Center was currently funding a salary for a daycare employee in another neighborhood and gave the name of the employee and the institution.

The administrator looked her straight in the face and said, "No."

Kelley's eyes dilated and her face set in a hard mask. The making of a radical.

Don asked again what the office *would* be willing to do for us, say after we were incorporated and had our board of directors. Would they put pressure on the city, for instance?

The administrator was evasive. She seemed to imply they might make a few phone calls.

I asked if they could pressure the university to provide space for our daycare program because that resource would virtually assure city funding. The administrator immediately started complaining about Teachers College. The troubles the university had had with that institution! It would be a step in the right direction if we could pressure them to do something. This was their field. They never pulled their own weight and it was such a shame.

Then some way or other we were out the door, all of us shaking hands. The administrator asked her secretary in a tired voice if she could come in now so they could get through those letters.

Don and Kelley and I were out on the street. My mind was reeling. All I could think of was: they did it to me again. They had softened my brain and I hadn't even protested. I just sat there and let all that institutionalese steamroll over me. And the children still had their same old needs. And the Urban Center still had its millions.

Don was amused. Seeing a money hustle from the inside was at least interesting. Don and I estimated our chances of getting money out of the Urban Center at about 39,751 to 2. He talked about a youth program he had worked in the summer before. They had worked out so many problems and everything was running smoothly, but the funds were stopped. He wondered what those kids were going to be doing this summer, out on the street.

Kelley was very depressed. None of that money was going to get into the community of Morningside Heights *or* Harlem. Harlem was Columbia University's community. That was so funny, I couldn't even laugh. I wondered if other people at the university knew that Harlem was their community. I wondered if people in Harlem knew that they were part of the university's community. I wondered if the alumni knew.

"Well, Kelley, at least we got some sound professional advice. And if we did all the things she suggested, we could keep busy for at least another year before she even had to meet with us again to give us more advice."

That one didn't go over well, either. Kelley said good-bye and walked off home by herself.

In a few days the effects of the meeting should have worn off enough so that we could get back to our prime need: space for the children. But we couldn't get back on the track that easily. Kelley and I both wasted a lot of energy finding out where that Urban Center/Ford Foundation money was going. It wasn't so awful. Just typical. None of the money for the community got to the community. Most of it went back into the office itself. The rest went directly to Columbia University to fund special chairs and outside lecturers who could prove some connection with urban problems and to establish the Bureau of Applied Research Study of Columbia University. The bureau made studies on the community for the university and filed reports helpful to the university. In addition the Urban Center funded a few conferences so the learned could discuss urban affairs.

So now we knew, but knowing didn't change anything. The space was there. The children were there. We decided the president of the university was the person to talk to, and that was the first problem. There was no way that Kelley and I could talk to him. The board of trustees owned his office in Low Library and his mansion on 116th Street and Morningside Drive and they hired men to guard both pieces of property. The men were given official uniforms, walkie-talkies, billy clubs, and explicit instructions to keep outsiders out.

We couldn't talk to the president and he wasn't even in charge. He was just another employee who collected his salary every Friday and tried not to get fired. The fringe benefits were too good to lose. The board of trustees was in charge. The board members were experienced men, substantial citizens, who knew about real estate and banking and how to run a big business. They were twenty men who, as executive officers, directors, and consultants, together, in various combinations, helped run CBS, the *New York Times*, Time Inc., the Chemical Bank, Banker's Trust, Manufacturer's Hanover Trust, Greenwich Savings Bank, Chase Manhattan, Lockheed, the Institute for Defense Analysis, the Defense Department, the U.S. Army, Con Edison, Allied Chemical, IBM, Shell Oil, AT&T, Standard Oil, more banks, life insurance companies, Uris real estate, Revlon, Chock Full O'Nuts, Pentagon war research, the District Attorney's office, the Rockefeller Foundation, the Ford Foundation, and with their business associates, friends, and acquaintances also ran the university, Morningside Heights, the city, and a great deal of the rest of the world.

The university was one institution that wouldn't have any trouble getting funded the second or third year. Of course, there were some problems with the students. A conflict of interests between them and the trustees. Nothing terribly serious, and anyway, the students were all gone every four years, and the trustees stayed forever.

Our group knew about the trustees. But we repressed this knowledge. It was easy. We announced that we would run through that institution faster than they could give us the runaround and that we would go directly to the top rung of the hierarchy—that no one, no one would stop us. And then Kelley and I argued with Todd about whether we should send our letter to the president or to a more responsive person further down the hierarchy. Todd's point was that the president was not going to concern himself with the problems of a bunch of women and children, and that we should go through channels from the bottom, reaching the top only if it became necessary. Todd was right. The president wouldn't care about the children or us and neither would the officials at the neighborhood churches or the officials at funding agencies or the officials working for the city. That truth made my stomach nervous and I wanted to go home to bed and forget it, but Kelley was firm and so I was firm.

February 18: Our letter of request landed on the president's secretary's desk.

For two weeks the institution didn't move and we didn't move.

The fact that we were so dependent on their goodwill paralyzed us. Dependency stopped our thought processes. My irrational train of thought was back. It had been with me all through Nancy's six months of talks with the Presbyterian church and it went like this: Maybe if we didn't mention their empty space directly but just had a long friendly talk, some words would pass between us that would persuade, convince, make them want to give us space, because we were nice people and our children were nice, and our project was worthy, as everyone kept saying. But now a light bulb was beginning to flicker in my brain. There were many situations in which it didn't make any difference what we said or what we had to offer to benefit the community. We could say anything. The outcome was predetermined. Everyone would be very nice. They would steamroll over us and say good-bye. And if we were lucky and persistent and followed all their rules, they would, out of the goodness of their hearts, allow us to build ourselves another institution that we didn't want and in only another year or two or three. And the institutionalists could then clasp their hands with pride and say "We've done it to them so long, now they can do it themselves." And if we objected, they would be offended and say that was a sign of our incompetence. Just thinking about it made me mad. We absolutely had to stop worrying about how we could please the institutions and where we fitted in and what they could do for us or to us and start thinking about what we would do to them if they stopped us from doing something good for ourselves and our children. I told Kelley to phone the president immediately and ask him if he had found space for the children yet. She said we should wait a few more days. Unless I wanted to call him. We waited a few more days.

March 3: Kelley phoned the president's office requesting a reply. She was told the secretary was out.

March 4, 9:30 A.M.: The president's office phoned Kelley to say the letter had been referred to the assistant vice-president for physical planning at the university.

10:30: The assistant vice-president for physical planning phoned me to say he was in charge of physical space and that he didn't know if any physical space was available. I asked if he ever looked out his window or walked to his office from where he parked his car. He said if Mrs. Harlow was going to be hostile he wouldn't talk to her at all. (Keep the dialogue going and the channels of communication open. Try to keep your head together. Avoid parking meters. Enjoy schizophrenia.) He said that anyway, it was against the policy of the institution to allow an independent community group use of institutionally owned space. I mentioned an example where this policy was not enforced. I was polite. He said he didn't know anything about what I was talking about and that he would look into my request.

March 5: Kelley and I had a conference and decided *not* to deal with underlings appointed to get rid of us.

March 8: Kelley phoned the president's office to get an answer to our request. The secretary was out.

March 10: Kelley phoned the president's office to get an answer to our request. The substitute secretary wanted to know if we had any openings because her sister-in-law had a little girl and. . . . She said the real secretary would be back on Monday. She also asked Kelley to take her home phone number in case we got a place and could take more children.

March 14: Kelley phoned, etc. The secretary said there were several messages on her desk and didn't we know that the request had been referred, etc. More talk. She said she would look into it.

March 15, 9:30 A.M.: Kelley phoned, etc.

11:30: The assistant vice-president in charge of public relations phoned to say that he didn't know if any space was available but he had scheduled a meeting to look into it. The meeting was to be on March 20 at a place called Morningside Heights, Inc., the real estate arm of Columbia, which had been organized by David Rockefeller. (Among other holdings, the university owns the land under Rockefeller Center.)

11:45: Kelley and I had a conference about how we could make the institution give us a direct yes or no on the space. We had no intention of accepting a no answer, but it was best to know where we stood before another year had gone by. At all costs we had to avoid letting the conversation deteriorate into bureaucratic bullshit about our worthy project and our personal inadequacies. We had already let them put us off a month. We had to figure out our timetable and stick to it. They could meet with us forever and do nothing. We didn't have that kind of time, we had the children. Their first dodge was to keep repeating that they didn't know if any space was available. But we couldn't let them use that line now with so much space so abundantly, even offensively, apparent to the naked eye. Kelley and I formulated a plan.

12:30: Kelley and I started walking off the neighborhood, block by block. We noted all the vacant ground-floor space and asked the super or tenants who owned it. The answer was invariably the university. We thoroughly examined all the sites we could get into by a little heavy leaning on the door. We made notes.

4:30: Kelley phoned certain women who were secretaries in the institution to find out what they knew, off the record, about what was available.

7:30: I phoned friends in the neighborhood to find out what space was available in their buildings.

March 16, 10:00 A.M.: Nancy and I walked off more of the neighborhood, notebooks in hand.

4:30: Kelley and I went to see some tenants about our using the three vacant apartments on the ground floor of their building. They were for it. So much space. We could take care of 130 children. We could quadruple our budget. We could take care of poor women's children and working women's children. And to go with that: Quotas. Federal funding. City funding. Substantial citizens as board of directors. Overseeing the poor. Separating the child from the parent. Running a business. Sliding scales. Screening committees. And finally, planning sessions to try to think of ways to get the parents involved.

7:30–11:30: I received seventeen phone calls from various neighborhood women who had had their children check out that apartment downstairs by going down the fire escape and through the window, and women who had called a sister on 118th Street and she said two apartments were vacant at . . . and the sister had a friend in the housing office at Columbia and the sister called her friend and the friend said . . . and that other apartment was burned out eight years ago but the fire really was very minor, it was just an excuse to get the tenant out and the apartment was structurally sound and . . . and there was a whole building with all the fixtures on 121st Street off Amsterdam and there were other whole buildings at . . . and the whole first floor of . . . which the institution said they were going to use for a dormitory three years ago and never did.

12:00 midnight: I phoned Kelley. We pooled our information. We composed a letter to the president in which we listed five sites. All sites had been vacant for three to eight years, and all had bathroom facilities, were on the ground floor, were large enough to meet city requirements, and had two ground-floor exits to meet fire regulations. We suggested that in order to make the March 20 meeting a *working* meeting, the institution should decide before March 20 which of the five sites it wanted to make available for the use of the little children of the community.

March 17, 8:00 A.M.: Demi hand-delivered the letter on her way to class.

March 20, 1:30 P.M.: Kelley, Demi, Kay, Kathy, and I met at my home, which was around the corner from Morningside Heights, Inc., which was in turn within two and a half blocks of all of our proposed sites, and whose windows overlooked Morningside Park and all of Harlem. We decided that according to our timetable, we had to have use of a space by May 1 to make full use of the summer months before all those leggings and boots and sneakers and mufflers and colds set in to handicap us. We further decided that Kelley, who was going to law school in September, should be the one who would keep us strictly to the basic questions. Which site? Where did we have to go to get a key? We also decided to stick together and back each other up. No disagreements in public.

2:28: We marched out of my apartment building.

2:29: The director of Morningside Heights, Inc., shook hands with everyone and was genial. He then gave us a clipboard to sign our names and addresses. "Just to see if you live in the neighborhood, heh, heh."

The director's consultant arrived from his office in another part of M.H.I. A woman was there from an organization representing the local public schools. We were introduced to each other. Everyone seemed a little surprised to see us. After all, there was no other community on Morningside Heights anymore, only students and staff. That was a fact. All the Columbia brochures said so.

While we waited for the assistant vice-president for public affairs, the director of M.H.I. leaned against the front of his desk and explained just what Morningside Heights, Inc., was. Morningside Heights, Inc., was a coordinating body for the real estate interests of all the institutions on the Heights. Columbia, of course, but not just the university: it also included, among others, Riverside Church, Union Theological Seminary, Jewish Theological Seminary, Teachers College, St. Luke's Hospital, Women's Hospital, St. Hilda's and St. Hugh's schools, the Presbyterian church, and the Cathedral of St. John the Divine. The major part of the budget,

$100,000, was allotted for their private police force, the Morning-side Patrol. The director added that the office worked closely with the local precinct and liked to think of themselves as "the eyes and ears of the law."

On that cheery note, the assistant vice-president for public affairs walked in and we began our meeting.

The director's consultant was curious as to why we wanted to have a relationship with Harlem.

We said many of us had moved into the neighborhood five, six, ten years ago because it was integrated and now our children were forced to grow up in a white ghetto (titters from the men) and we didn't want that for our children or for us. This insular living condition was one of cultural deprivation (blank stares). The men changed the subject.

Kelley asked about our five sites.

The assistant vice-president for public affairs said that we had to understand that there were groups with higher priority and that his institution had faculty groups, student groups, and administration all continually seeking extra space and that we were on the list but would have to wait our turn.

I asked where on the list.

The assistant vice-president said we were about eighteenth.

Eighteenth. My mind raced. Who had higher priority than little children and it's about time that that humanistic institution started being humanistic and if they thought they could sit around another ten years hoarding all those 204 vacant rent-controlled apartments and all those storefronts, and evict more people, and tear down more housing and then put in little playgrounds that were immediately fenced and padlocked . . .

The director's consultant said something about how they had to put fences around the playgrounds because they had to lock them up one day a year to maintain their property rights. I said the 113th Street playground had been locked up since the middle of last summer. The director's consultant said that the institution had stopped funding an attendant's salary and that understandably the institution didn't want to be liable for . . . I said, as if I were playing Medea to an audience of thousands, "You mean you won't let my child slide down your sliding board." The director's consultant was yelling at me to be reasonable. Kay, who couldn't bear fights or aggression of any kind, almost yelled at me to shut up but ended by pleading with everyone to get back to the subject.

The director, an older, experienced executive, gave an almost angry look at the young and obviously inexperienced assistant vice-president, and smilingly assured the ladies present that they had very high priority, very, very high priority.

Kelley asked about our five sites.

The assistant vice-president gave a classic institutional reply. He was still rough but had certainly absorbed the basics. He was the embodiment of reason. It seemed that our request for space *directly* from the institution was not feasible and that he would encourage us *to explore all possibilities on a long-term basis*.

Kelley asked about our five sites.

Of course, the letter arrived too late to be considered for this meeting. The assistant vice-president didn't know if any of these sites was available. The letter had been turned over to the director of the Office of Neighborhood Services, who was going to look into it.

(This office's major neighborhood service for the past five years had been emptying the neighbors out of their homes so the institution could expand. The office's director was so good at this that the institution kept raising his salary. And best of all, he had no connection with anyone we were meeting with right now but was responsible to bosses in a hierarchy in a whole other division of the institutional corporation.)

Somehow, this man had not been invited to the meeting and no one there seemed to know much about him, except me, who had been personally removed with family from my home by the man two years ago. (As we were being evicted, the director of neighborhood services kept saying he was just doing his job and when it was all over he was hurt when Lester had refused to shake hands with him. Some people take personal things too personally.)

Kelley, Demi, and Kathy spent five minutes finding out who this man's boss was and who *his* boss was and who *his* boss was and then with general gloom descending over the assembled women (even the public school woman, who hadn't said one word in two hours but just took notes and more notes), Kelley suggested that we were in the wrong place and perhaps we should go to the director of neighborhood services' office and talk to him. Our troops were showing signs of strain.

The men leaped in with smiles, chuckles, assurances that we *were* in the right place. They could take care of this whole matter for us. If we would just let ourselves be helped. Then they all proceeded to offer us so many suggestions and helpful ideas that I was afraid we were going to be "niced" to death. First of all, we should stop concentrating on those five sites. How would we like to locate someplace out of Morningside Heights, say Manhattanville, that was an integrated neighborhood? We should really consider opening this thing up. We would get much further by not concentrating on the university, but what we should do is contact all sixteen institutions and really open up possibilities for ourselves. Why didn't we consider the possibility of taking a place for a couple of hours a day just for the summer?

Kelley asked about our five sites.

The assistant vice-president smiled. He wanted us to know that our research was a little faulty since the director of neighborhood services himself was living in one of our sites. Hahahaha. And, who knows, maybe our other sites had people living in them, too. Hehhehheh.

Kelley didn't move an eyelash. Could we have a letter in five days giving us an answer as to the availability of one of our five sites?

The assistant vice-president said yes.

We stood around and talked for a few minutes and that was it.

4:30: We sat around my living room. One of the women said she was surprised by the meeting, she had heard so many terrible things about the institution and those people were so nice. That statement depressed me for at least the next two and a half years.

Oh, it was true. The men were nice. I had seen so many institutional people who were nice. They spoke nicely. Good grammar. No swear words. Clean fingernails. Polished shoes. Polite words. Polite sympathy, up to a point. There were limits. Actual needs of actual children were not their concern.

There were two standard institutionalist responses. The first was laughter. Not at us but with us—which stopped only when the laugher saw we didn't have a sense of humor. The second response was one of world-weary patience. How could we bring up the subject of children as we did so crudely when the institutional person was trying to have a serious discussion with us? The institutional person was then doubly upset because he or she only wanted to help and he or she could see right now that we were going to get nowhere if we kept yapping about the children. After all, everyone is in favor of children. That's not the point.

But it was. We tried to tell them about real children, and they said what we *should* talk about was boards of directors, and bureaus and incorporation, and laws and statutes, and subsections, and lawyers, and how much we were going to have to pay in insurance fees to prevent (or encourage) our neighbors' suing us for all we were worth.

I had an image of Kelley and me building snowmen with the children. The children wanted to throw snowballs but being hit by one was a little too scary at their age so Kelley and I said they could throw snowballs at us. Throwing something at mommy, as long as she keeps laughing, may be the all-time greatest nursery activity—guaranteed to inspire total participation, amazing sibling cooperation, and most of all, joy.

I had a second image of Kelley and me out of our jeans and into dresses at official meetings. The two images didn't mesh. Lying in bed late at night, I had to keep trying to remember why we were doing this.

March 21: First of all, the director of neighborhood services did not live in one of our sites. It was empty and he was storing his family's bicycles there. I knew my friend's sister's children could be trusted to get the facts. Kelley and I sat in her living room and plotted. If the letter agred to our use of one site we would move in with the children, ask more families to join us, and have community daycare. That would be the end, or one could say the beginning.

The second and more likely alternative was that the institution would refuse to share. A refusal on March 25 was going to necessitate some quick moving on our part to get an acceptance before May 1. It was, first of all, necessary to extricate ourselves from this chain of underlings and get to see the president himself. So when we got our letter of refusal, we would quickly write another letter refusing the refusal and rush it up the street to the president, whom we would demand to see personally and in public. We meaning all the mothers in our group, all the children, some of the fathers, mothers, and children from other nurseries in the neighborhood, students from the university, old friends from tenant battles, several family dogs, and at least three newborn babies.

Kelley got on the phone. Todd got more and more nervous. He kept saying that the institution would never ever give us space. I kept saying that they certainly were going to give us space and it would be very good for them to have to do it.

Todd said that I was naive. Couldn't I see that the institution wanted to get rid of us? If we weren't careful we were just going to alienate them and then we'd never get anything. I said he should worry about how the institutions were alienating us. Anyway, we weren't stupid, we knew they didn't care about children or parents or daycare and the institutions knew it, but they could never say it in public—and that's where we had them. That's where every mother and every child in the city had every church, school, and public institution. If these human service institutions ever considered the needs of the children, they would have offered space already, even squeezed up a little to make room. The space was there and the children should have it. And mothers were just the people to get it for them. In ten years children would have their own little place on every block in the city.

Kelley continued making phone calls. Todd became even more nervous.

March 24: The assistant vice-president for public affairs phoned Kelley to ask for an extension of time. He said an extension was in our best interests. Kelley said he must reply at the agreed time.

March 25: Deadline day. The letter began with a preface written by the assistant which spoke of our worthwhile and beneficial project and said the institution was committed to "cooperate in any reasonable and practical way within our means." The core of the letter was a repeat of the director of neighborhood services' report, which listed the five sites with a reason for refusal after each one. Three of the reasons for refusal were outright lies and two were suspicious. The assistant ended the letter with his regrets about the director's findings and told us to drop him a note if we were still interested in pursuing the subject. We could be assured of the institution's continued interest.

But we didn't want their regrets or their interest. We wanted a place for the children. So Kelley and I carefully composed our letter of refusal of their refusal, asking the president for a tour of the five sites. The march on the president's office in Low Library was definitely on for the day after tomorrow.

Todd went straight to the president's office to try to head this thing off and get everyone together for a reasonable talk. He was refused an appointment. Kelley wrote a leaflet asking everyone to come and join our demonstration. One of the mothers translated it into Spanish and it was mimeographed on both sides of the paper.

March 26: Mothers' phones were ringing. Women plotted on street corners with their arms full of groceries. We would meet in Low Plaza tomorrow at noon. Bring the children. Bring everybody you can.

Todd went to the president's office again. He was refused admittance. The president was taping a radio interview about the "new" university's wonderful community relations.

March 27, 8:30 A.M.: Todd made a last attempt to see the president. No dice.

10:00: Kelley and Constance and Demi and Kathy and I leafleted the neighborhood announcing our demonstration. This activity was nerve-racking. We thought surely someone would read the leaflet and try to stop us. But the institutional people were all in their institutional offices and we were out on the street.

12:00–1:30: We assembled. Kay brought lots of paper and crayons and paints. It was cold and the wind kept blowing the papers away. The children were still in their snowsuits. They painted large signs for themselves demanding space for a daycare program. Kelley Marie and Billy held hands for three hours. Several people brought food and we had lunch. One mother brought her guitar and we sang "Three Blind Mice" and "Down at the Station." Our ranks were decimated. Bootsie and Sean had the chicken pox and Nancy was home with both of them. Sean had broken out very badly and seemed to be suffering more than was usual. A couple of women from our own group didn't show up because they were against our tactics. We should not alienate the institution. They were firm on this point. They said it was a disgrace to demonstrate. And with children. They also said they hoped we got a place. Todd and Lester showed up and some neighbors without children, and some people from the Community Action Committee, which had recently died from the exhaustion of fighting long-established institutions and of internal political debates. We had a five-minute strategy meeting. All the parents are the staff and administration of the Children's Free School, so all the parents, in fact, everybody here should meet with the president, even the children. No division of our numbers. The institution kept issuing statements that it wanted community relations, so we'll give it community relations. We will calmly and politely deliver the letter to the president and then we will simply stay there in his office till we get an affirmative reply. In fact, his office would make a dandy daycare center in the interim. The bathroom, according to reliable sources, was one of the best in the city.

Visibility was a factor. Institutional people just didn't seem to be able to connect a demand for daycare facilities with the actual real live babies who would be using those facilities. There was nothing like confrontation with those babies in the flesh. They were just at the right age to make all their needs bluntly and forcefully and interminably apparent.

We gathered in more or less of a group.

There was a commotion in the back. People were calling me. It was Whitney. Demi pushed Whitney's bangs aside to show me one giant red and yellow chicken pox. Lester and I and Demi and some other women talked it over. Whitney stayed.

The march proceeded slowly up the stairs to the doors. Most of the children needed their hands held.

The uniformed men guarding the entrances talked frantically into their walkie-talkies. They told Kelley, who was holding our letter, that we could not come in, absolutely under no circumstances. Kathy argued with them. They argued back. Her son, Philip, was yanking on Kathy's coat. He was cold and he had to go to the bathroom and he was bored with all this talking so he went right through the guard's legs and took off for the ladies' room on his own. Edmund went through the guard's legs, too. Several other children tried, but the guard readjusted his stance, so they went around. There was even a feeble attempt by a couple of parents to say, "Hey, the man said you couldn't do that." But then somebody had to go after Philip and Edmund and in about two minutes we were all inside and the guards were still telling us we couldn't be there. From that point, it was all downhill for the institution.

Philip and Constance came back from the bathroom. A couple of women sat all the children down on stair steps in the giant marble foyer and launched them into the first of what turned out to be 103 verses of "I Know an Old Woman Who Swallowed a Fly."

The vice-president for business appeared to handle us. Of course we could see the president. The vice-president for business himself would be glad to make an appointment for some of us at a later date. What was the name of our group?

There was a strident, strained, nearly hostile attempt to break through to this man. We are here now. We are standing in front of you right now. We want to see the president right now. All of us. Every person came here, because every person here wants to talk to the president. Now. That's why we came.

The vice-president for business seemed to change a bit. The president, he said, wasn't in his office, wasn't available, but *he* would see us.

The crucial question. Do you have power to permit the community to use institutionally owned space?

The crucial answer. Yes.

The vice-president for business disappeared with our letter in hand, to hunt up the assistant vice-president for public affairs.

Lester rushed off to a phone booth to call the newspapers. "Thirty three-year-olds have just taken over Low Library. No, not thirty-three-year-olds. I said three-year-olds. Yes. Three-year-olds." (The university had big media value and the various media representatives had competitive clocked times from their front offices to Low Plaza.)

The vice-president for business returned with the assistant vice-president for public affairs, who appeared to be in the first stages of shock, and I had the distinct impression that the assistant vice-president for public affairs had just suffered a tongue-lashing, more intense than anything remembered from grammar school days.

The children were well into "I Know an Old Woman," and the grownups were forced to shout at each other. Both institutional representatives were extremely nervous, almost trembling, because of all the children, and because of the song, and because of all the adults, none of whom could be put in a convenient category. Mostly they were visibly upset because they had yet to institutionalize the things to say in this kind of situation.

The vice-president for business made another attempt to take one or two of us off to his office and meet alone.

No.

An adjoining rotunda was quickly filled with folding chairs. We all met together. At least seven or more of the grownups there were quite vocal and the meeting was just a replay of all the points we had been making all along. But the tone was different.

For the first time we were taken seriously. No evasions. No paternalism. The vice-president took notes on what we were saying. He had to be affirmative because there was nothing left. In my opinion, there were three strong reasons why the institution was dead set against us. We were an independent community group and letting us use some of their property would be setting up a possible hazard to their property rights. A very dangerous precedent for absentee ownership of property all over the world. Second, we would quite likely stir up the tenants in any building we were allowed to use, thereby making it more difficult for the institution to evict them when their time came. And worse than both of these reasons, we wanted to include black mothers and black children in our group and the institution didn't want any more strife with the black community. The institution had been so nice about the gym in Morningside Park and look where that got them. The great thing about all these reasons was that none of them could be said in public. I almost wanted to grin. We were also blessed with our image, young mothers and their little babies, and if we weren't black or on welfare, we were up there on a pedestal, at least in public where people were taking our pictures. The vice-president for business read his notes back to the group to be sure he was correct in his understanding. He had agreed to arrange for us to tour the five sites. He had agreed to the community's use of vacant space for daycare, and before May 1.

The assistant vice-president for public affairs said again he knew nothing about the five sites.

The vice-president for business said he knew nothing about these five sites.

Lester was smart enough near the end of the meeting to ask the vice-president for business to write us a letter immediately saying that the institution had agreed to give use of vacant space to the Children's Free School.

The vice-president for business was flustered by this suggestion but the newspaper reporters were there taking pictures of the children and of us and of him and he said yes, of course. We disbanded with the vice-president for business following me to the door saying that the institution was firmly behind us and even approved of our worthy project, but that we should be careful not to associate with people like that. He pointed to two students who had stationed themselves silently at the back of the room during the meeting. The vice-president for business just wanted to warn us. If we associated with people like that it would hurt our worthy cause. We should be careful who we hung around with.

I told him, politely, that I had to go see about my daughter's chicken pox.

An old and dear friend, Richard, came chugging up to Low Plaza on his bicycle, loaded down with fifty or sixty Dixie cups of ice cream. Everyone ate in the sun and congratulated each other. By God, we had done it. We had broken through the institutional diffusion. Everybody was celebrating. Lester and I took Whitney home and put her to bed with two Dixie cups of vanilla.

5.   A Storefront Is Ours

The vice-president's letter never came. Kelley phoned him. He whined. We were to be assured that the institution was as committed to the children as ever, but there was some doubt about his putting it in writing because, you see, lawyers could then use that piece of paper to force the institution to give space to our group and although his institution was totally committed to our project . . .

Kelley was insistent.

The next day the assistant for public affairs handed us the vice-president's letter. Completed, I was convinced, only after long hours of sweaty toil, the document was the ultimate expression of the noncommitment of commitment. While our group was still recovering from the heady experience of encountering perfection in prose, the assistant, who was meeting with us to tour the five sites, explained that we were not going to tour the five sites.

They never gave up.

We yelled at him and at another official accompanying him. The assistant said they had two other sites in mind and if we didn't go to see them we wouldn't be seeing anything.

Keep the channels of communication open. Keep a dialogue going. Why?

The first site was impossible for small children. Up three flights of steep stairs and with the second exit out a window and down three flights of rickety fire escape. The second site was possible. A storefront on Morningside Drive. Holes in the floor. No kitchen. Two ground-floor exits. There was general dilapidation and filth from being vacant for a couple of years. Twenty-five to thirty children would be a maximum capacity.

Kelley asked about our five sites.

They glared at her. It was so difficult for them, having to deal with this hostility. Don't you people ever trust anybody? For your information, the university's newly hired master planner, not him personally but the master planner's office, has all those sites under intensive study and they are to be converted to housing in the near future.

The officials added in deep growls that they were sure we would be happy about that.

We were. But it turned out to be a lie. We found that out by calling the master planner's office.

They said, "What five sites?" and "Never heard of them."

Nice people. Liked kids, had some of their own. They *wanted* community contacts. Coexistence was one answer to the institution's problems. That, and better utilization of the space the university already owned, and building up instead of out, and building multifunctional structures. The people in the planning office were excited about talking to us. Us, an authentic grass-roots community group running a daycare program. This could be an example of what could be done: we would run the daycare center, the institution would lend the space, and the university could be socially useful in the community without the draining responsibility of financial loss.

The master planners were behind us, had influence, and we at last were going to get space for our daycare center. They went with us to the real estate office to pick up the keys to the five sites. The university real estate people wouldn't give the master planners the keys. The master planners were embarrassed and giggled, then they got angry. Phone calls, hostilities, going to higher-ups, swearing, telling the wife the new story about that impossible place. It took them three days to get the keys.

We explored our prime site, three apartments on the ground floor of 130 Morningside Drive, rent-controlled, seven rooms each, enormous space. We made estimates of renovation costs, imagined where there could be a quiet room, where we could hang the trapeze and the swing, and where we would keep the blocks. Kelley was talking of 130 children again, city, state, and federal funds, and a full professional staff eventually, and, of course, no change in our closeness with the children. A nice dream.

A few days later one of the people at the master planner's office answered the telephone and a lot of rage came out. It was our committed friend from the university, the vice-president for business. In essence his message was, off the record, that all of this daycare business was none of the master planners' g.d. business and they should get the hell out of it. Also they should remember that they were hired by the university, *not* the community.

So the master planners got the hell out of it. A year and a half later they submitted their master plan and were promptly fired by the university's board of trustees.

For us, there were more meetings with the institution. More pettiness. More lies and half-truths on their part or just confusing bureaucracy. Much more. The sites might be housing someday, true, but not for community people. The assistant was friendlier. But it was obvious that he had little power. And the institution was filled with such people. Over the past two months Kelley and I had talked with so many decent, understanding institutional people who were just doing their jobs that we were left in a state of total immobility.

I was discouraged, depressed, and very tired. I didn't know what Kelley was feeling because I never talked to her anymore. It wasn't only the interminable institutional quagmire we were immersed in. There were the children. We also had to take care of them on our day and every night and twenty-four hours a day on weekends.

Jinx still wrote up her trips in the big black book. Jane and Marilyn wrote about popping corn and making pancakes with the children and a new game where they all pretended they were ducks. Kelley and I hadn't made an entry for two months. We were moving through our time with the children like zombies. We had been sucked in.

Our group's function was to share child rearing. What we were doing now was attending a succession of "important" meetings with "important" officials. The officials were content to meet with us, often and at length. It was their job.

These men lived in one world—the world of the job, the career. Children were excluded. Even thoughts of children were excluded from that world. It certainly made their meetings with us easier for them. We were rushing back and forth from one world to another and not doing so well in either. While their mothers talked real estate and rules and regulations and law and who said what to whom, our children continued to be shuttled around the neighborhood and were no closer to having a permanent shelter over their heads. It didn't look as if we were going to make it out of those meetings and into a space. Time was always on the side of the institutions. The longer they could keep us negotiating, the less chance we had of actually making a neighborhood daycare center. Half of us were exhausted most of the time, including the time we were with the children. We had become so involved in the daycare quagmire, justifying our need for existence, pleading, threatening, that the children were becoming a secondary consideration. I mean, we were doing all of this for them but now we had less and less time to be with them. The American way.

Somewhere in the midst of this Kelley and I exhausted ourselves —emotionally, physically, institutionally. I stopped cold. Kelley, too. We didn't rush to the children, hold them against our breasts, and sing the ABCs to them. We did nothing. It was on one of those depressing days in late April as I was lying on the sofa, looking at the cracks in the ceiling and wondering how I could extend my sleeping time from fourteen to twenty hours a day, when the doorbell rang and Constance came whirling into the apartment like a tornado screaming, "I got the key!"

If there's one thing about our group that I am always and eternally grateful for, it's the fact that it's a group. That morning Constance got up in a foul mood, brooded through two hours' reading of Engels' *The Family, Private Property, and the State* and after thoroughly convincing herself that enough was enough, she marched over to the office of the assistant vice-president for public affairs and told him to get on the phone and get a release for the key to 76 Morningside Drive. We were taking one of the two sites they had offered us: the storefront with holes in the floor and no kitchen. She made him promise to install a kitchen. He said word of honor. Constance made him say it twice, and then she remembered to get it in writing.

We were well out of that world. At all those meetings no one had mentioned children once. Institutional people spent their lives worrying over property rights and money rights and double-talking about "exploring wider possibilities" and "making resources available." They had built themselves an enormous superstructure of official channels and words and paper and spent all their days holding it all up.

I called Kelley and she was happy, sort of. At least it was over. The place could never be a service center for 130 children. In a small storefront with our own children and a few more neighborhood families the chances for funding or professional teachers or screening committees weren't too good.

We had failed and I was relieved.

6.   The Village Builds Its Nursery for Free (Plus $200)

The entrance to our storefront was on Morningside Drive—down some stairs in a basement. Next to the front door was a big plate-glass window with another around the corner on 118th Street. The cramped dark inner area was divided by pasteboard walls into cubbyhole offices with a long dark hall alongside. The rooms were filled with institutional stuff covered with filth, huge gray pieces of metal office furniture, numerous disconnected telephones, large bundles of ripped-out telephone wires, a Xerox machine, and twenty or thirty dirty boxes containing thousands of copies of bureaucratic reports, old and clean and unread. In the center of the storefront was a kitchen area with exposed pipes and wires where the fixtures used to be and a tiny bathroom with a broken toilet. Few of the overhead lights worked and there were holes in the floor. What we had at the end of a heavy struggle was an incredible dump, but most of us adamantly refused to see that. We looked over, around, and through the reality and saw only the future— that there would be a neighborhood daycare facility where none had been before.

Our immediate objective was to move the children into that space fast, before some official put in a veto or wrote a new rule. We phoned each family to get ready for action. The first weekend we piled the pieces of institutional hulk floor to ceiling in the last room to the back and with mops, brooms, sponges, and shovels, began salvaging one room at a time.

Kay lugged a formica tabletop in out of the garbage. I bought some short legs for it, and Constance and I screwed them on. Jinx brought in some little chairs. Someone else brought milk crates and the children were in their school in three days. Equipment consisted of a few puzzles, crayons and paper, and all our blunt-edged scissors from home. Lunches and snacks were brought in and we had picnics every day. The first week we took the children on trips—across the street to the sandbox, down three streets to the playground, and around the block to see where their school was in relation to the rest of the world.

Lisa's father painted CHILDREN'S FREE SCHOOL on the front door. Edmund's father changed the lock and his mother made fifteen copies of the key and gave one to each family. It was our school.

At least the location was what we had wanted—Morningside Drive, across from Harlem. We were a few blocks from 125th Street, where the two public schools enrolled a high percentage of black and Puerto Rican children, with younger brothers and sisters.

Jane worked the first day we were open. The next day her daughter, Vivien, didn't come to school. Thursday, no Vivien. Friday, no Vivien. Jane called me on Saturday. She and Vivien were dropping out. She said her husband wouldn't let her work on Morningside Drive—too dangerous up there. Then Jane's friend Marilyn stopped me in the dime store. She and Jeff were dropping out. Her husband said the neighborhood was too dangerous for them.

Kelley took Marilyn's place that week. I covered for Jane. Then Blanche came in two hours late and Kay had to cover for her. The school had barely gotten under way and we were already fighting to hold things together.

Constance was in charge of admissions and scheduling, busily admitting nearly everyone that walked in off the street. There was space to share, vacant spots in our schedule, and a need for volunteer heavy labor. The last was most important because we were going to create and run a school without money.

A group called Urban Deadline, made up of radical architects from the university's School of Architecture, volunteered to measure the storefront and make scale drawings. We talked about big open spaces for the children to run in, in contrast to the confining apartment rooms, and about sunshine, and about simplicity in design and lack of clutter, and after talking and talking and talking we came up with a plan. There would be four broad areas: a noisy place for running, jumping, dancing, screaming, wrestling, climbing, swinging, and messing around with friends; a small room with a door for playing house, hospital, fire station, witch's cave, and for telling secrets; a utilitarian area, kitchen, bathroom, and storage for those things potentially dangerous to children. A large separate room with a door would be the quiet room, for painting, reading and telling stories, doing puzzles, counting, playing with clay, and taking naps.

To get any sunshine or open any large areas we had to get rid of some of those pasteboard walls. Don't touch anything—especially the walls!—is the word from the institution. There are procedures to follow if we want to make changes in the property. The procedure is to apply in writing for permission from the real estate properties men. We are certainly entitled to follow this procedure, but, the administrators are quick to add, we will be turned down, definitely and absolutely, because the men who are to give us permission resent our existence and have vowed never to give us permission to do anything ever. Constance's husband, an expatriate Englishman and an assistant professor at the university, had given his word to the assistant vice-president for public affairs that we would not lay a hand on any of their walls. Kelley's husband agreed. The institution owned the storefront and their property rights superseded all other considerations.

At the storefront both husbands were telling us that the walls should stay up and if we had any thoughts of going ahead with tearing them down we better get that out of our minds and if we touched those walls we would be very sorry and they would bear no responsibility for such an act and then Ian and Todd left. Constance and Kelley and Kathy and I sat and stared at the plasterboard wall running the width of the back room. The plasterboard wall had a door in it, locked, no trace of a key anywhere in the university conglomerate.

Constance looked at the wall and was philosophical. She said it was the same with her landlord, he always thought the apartment was his because he owned it and she always thought the apartment was hers because she lived there. She said the walls should come down. I looked at the wall and talked about function. The walls had gone up years ago to make rooms for administrators; they should come down now to make rooms for children. Kathy was practical. She said if we were going to do it we better do it before the men came back. Ian and Todd had been gone only five minutes when the four of us had hammers in our hands and the back-room wall was on its way down. Destroying a wall is fun. We got happier and happier with every blow. Behind where the wall used to be we discovered another fifty square feet of space, three magazines dated

October and November 1947, old wooden desks and folding chairs, camping and photographic equipment from the period, and a large rusty sink whose faucet had evidently been dripping for twenty-two years.

By the time Ian and Todd got back and more fathers arrived, we were in a roaring good humor and there were many more women eager to break walls. They started in on the front. The men stayed out of it, denied all responsibility for such an unregulated act, and Ian worried about his reputation and rehearsed his speech to the administration. "Personally, I disclaim any responsibility. You know these women, there's no controlling these women."

We put the walls in seventeen large garbage cans and the city sanitation department brought a special truck and took them away.

A woman walked in off the street to see what was going on. She was astounded. City people can barely imagine walls being built by construction workers and it jars their equilibrium to see plain old everyday run-of-the-mill people take a wall down with their bare hands. She couldn't believe we could do it ourselves. Wouldn't the whole building fall in? She also couldn't believe that we had no director, that we were going to offer free daycare, that the place was rent-free, that all the families were going to teach, and even the children; that we had been running a daycare operation out of our apartments, and that we had started our group three days after our first meeting. She roamed around the place saying, "You people are great. You people are really great. I can't believe you people." Good old Marion, we'd never seen her before in our lives, but we loved her.

She had a degree in early education and had taught nursery school, and was full of ideas for changes in the nursery school structure, but she had never thought that people could just put their ideas to work. Marion had twin sons, not eligible for entrance to the Teachers College nursery, where she worked mornings. They were admitted and she signed up to teach in the Children's Free School two afternoons a week.

The real estate administrators tried to punish us for tearing down the walls without their permission. We had repeatedly requested removal of their office furniture and other possessions from the premises. Now they said that since we had not cooperated they would continue to store *their* office furniture, which was stacked three desks high in the back room, in *their* storefront indefinitely.

We told them they had three days or their property was going out on the street. Workers from Buildings and Grounds came the following day and removed everything.

Which finally gave Ian room to work. Ian and his friend Ashley love to build. Ashley was a dropout architect in the Urban Deadline group and with them not only worked without pay but supplied the necessary tools and hardware.

Building for these children had its special joys. The children had nothing in their new nursery and were terribly appreciative. When the climbing thing was placed in the center of the front room, Ian's son announced over and over again that *his* father built it and it would last forever. The climbing thing was a big rectangular wooden unit put together with bolts. Horizontally it was a fantasy boat or a submarine or bus or hiding place. Turned end for end it became a ladder and swinging bars and a place to stand to be taller than everybody else. Ian, who was in and out of the school at least three times a week now, could see that his creation was the first thing new children climbed onto, went under, jumped off of, and that it did last, and that his children and everyone else's children could play on the climbing thing every day for years and years. Satisfaction.

Ashley cut the legs of a heavy wooden table to children's height, sliced it in half, cut half circles in the center of each half and epoxied it all back together around one of the poles in the back room. A bench with a high back was built to fit along two sides of the table and the entire unit could turn in any direction.

The table had been a street discard. The gutters of New York City are filled with usable goods. Most of our lumber for building came from the streets and all of our tables and bookcases. Ian built two long paint easels out of recycled lumber and put them on either side of the back-room sink. All the shelving was recycled wood.

Ashley thought of building a sliding board out of plywood and two-by-fours. Ian bought new lumber and they stayed up till three A.M. one Sunday finishing it.

A couple walked up through Morningside Park from Harlem one Sunday and saw us all painting. They enrolled their son and spent the next evening painting the climbing thing orange because they liked that color.

The worker decided how the work should go. That was part of the joy of working. Our rule: the painter decided the colors she wanted to paint, the builder decided the size and shape of the built object, and the person cleaning decided what and how to clean. New people tried to find the person in charge and sometimes had difficulty adjusting to making their own decisions. From the beginning we had recognized the right of a woman to make decisions concerning her labor and had rejected the idea of leaders as impractical. Promoting leaders strengthened a few people and our aim was to strengthen the whole group by making everyone powerful.

In the case of converting the storefront there were frequent consultations with whoever was nearby at the time, but a group decision at this level was unwieldly, time-consuming, and unnecessary. The laborer was on her own as long as no bills were turned in at the end of the job.

We could see the storefront changing. There was continual surprise and delight at the individual accomplishments—and sometimes dismay.

Constance and Demi wanted to build, but lacked the necessary experience with building tools and the necessary masculinity to be easily accepted in this domain. Ian put up with them with some distaste. He listened to the feminist proclamations: no longer would men create while women cleaned up after them; women would create for their own personal satisfaction; it would be good for their daughters (and sons) to see them as creators. Ian said that was all very well, but obviously the time for women to learn basic carpentry skills was at sixteen, not at thirty—and not here. Several women did manage to do some carpentry work, but we accomplished no amazing leaps into equality in that area.

It was enough for Ian to deal with the men. He was amazed—and irked—at the number of men who couldn't pound a nail. He was even more amazed when several of these men undertook the most difficult carpentry jobs, all of which he had to redo in their absence. Also Ian's standards didn't allow a "window dressing" approach to converting the storefront. Preparing to paint was half the work, patching the plaster, taping edges, papering the floor to prevent drips, all this was an obvious necessity. I came in and painted a whole wall right over all the nails and two pieces of Scotch tape and one small hole, just like the professionals who painted my apartment every three years. I felt a wonderful sense of accomplishment. Somebody painted the kick boards pink. Another person went so far as to paint right over a child's painting that was Scotch-taped to the wall and someone else painted the top of the lunch table with water-based paint which dissolved when milk and juice were spilled on it and was washed away in a few days. Numbers of people rushed in, did an hour's worth of painting, and rushed out, leaving paintbrushes filled with paint, paint cans open, and spots on the floor, all for Ian to take care of. There was a further irritation. Ian bought what he considered were necessities and when he attempted to collect for them he found himself left with the larger share of the bill. The group was definitely not a collective, never entirely fair, at best was a conglomeration of individualists who tried to put up with each other, work together, and share, because of the children.

Ian did have Ashley and other skilled friends to help him and because they were there, instead of hanging a few hooks and baskets for the children's winter coats and hats, cubbies were made. Twenty of them. Cubbies are the traditional daycare center clothes closet. They are wooden rectangles four feet by two feet, with a shelf a foot from the top and large hooks in each side wall. The cubbies were placed at various angles in the front room to form little playing and working areas. The backs of the cubbies made four-foot walls, which was all the children needed. The builders also put up a wall to complete the fantasy room, built a bench along the outside wall and bookshelves along the inside, and even hung a door so the children could have their fantasies in private.

Some people didn't work on the storefront. The commitment to the school varied from person to person, but there was a minimum: everyone had to take care of everyone else's children for a certain period once a week.

We had been told that equipment wouldn't be a problem, and it wasn't. We had told our friends that we had a place for the children but nothing to put in it and we needed everything. That, and the fact that we existed solely for the children and in spite of the landlord, was a rallying cry to our neighbors.

The Garcías, across 118th Street, brought twenty milk crates which we used for chairs and tables and storage. The Savages, who lived upstairs over the school, brought in a beautiful hand-crafted dollhouse that had been made for their three teenage daughters when they were small. Another neighbor brought in a gallon of left-over orange paint.

Kay made suggestions for craft materials and people went through their homes and brought what they could, empty egg crates, scraps of material, buttons, toothpicks, old Christmas cards, and a variety of weird little objects to use for collages. Kathy brought in two used air conditioners.

Ian wrote to the assistant vice-president for public affairs requesting new plumbing. Only someone like Ian could write a letter about our storefront bathroom and manage to bring in the Nuremberg trials. The assistant vice-president was particularly dismayed at the accusation that he was endangering the health of the children. To which Ian replied something about our appreciation of his attempt to "bridge the Kafkan gulf that divides the Castle from the village." Ian said that we were to blame ourselves for allowing the bureaucracy to provide so many reasons for not correcting the stench and desolation that had become our bathroom. The bathroom was fixed. Shortly thereafter the assistant vice-president came by with a gallon of paint tied up in a satin ribbon. And six weeks later he called to tell us he was getting new carpet in his office and offered us his old carpet. It was barely worn industrial carpet, covered three-quarters of the school, and survived another four years with thirty children tromping over it and occasionally stomping peanut butter and jelly sandwiches into it.

To contact strangers we made a sign two feet wide and four feet long and put it in the window.

We need:
books
toys
wagons
tricycles
doll carriages
guitar
record player
piano
enamel paint
paintbrushes
rollers
brooms
vacuum cleaner
hammers
nails
saws
tools
and money

An official administrative-looking black man in a gray flannel suit came by one morning carrying a briefcase and two tricycles under his arm. He left the tricycles. A very old man came to the door with his broken alarm clock in a rumpled brown sack. We were offered three pianos and five record players. And we were given several used vacuum cleaners that only worked another week before they gave out. People brought in more dress-up clothes than we could use, and books, many of them too adult for our children, and puzzles, some sturdy wooden kinds and some cardboard ones that lasted a week if we were lucky, and toy soldiers and other toys kept for grandchildren who had now grown up or moved away.

The children were impressed at seeing their parents working so hard. That hard work was strengthening our group. The more personal effort put out, the less likely that the group would disintegrate. The school would exist because of our efforts. There was pride in that and a great deal of commitment. I wanted the children to feel that pride; to feel they were making a school, too.

I tried to organize the children to paint. They were eager. The parents were aghast. They didn't want to paint with the children. They didn't even want to be in the same room with three- and four-year-olds and cans of enamel paint. Ian was the most aghast. Because it was obvious that children and real paint don't mix. The men's major plea was to get the children out of the way so they could work. And I kept trying to push the children in the way. The adults said no. My daughter and I stayed after school one night and painted the sliding board red. Whitney was unbelievably excited, then quit after five minutes.

The children tried to give. They brought toys and books from home, though often they got so upset when another child touched their contribution that they had to take it back home again, sometimes for just a few days, sometimes forever.

A man walked in off the street to talk about the school. He was middle-aged, white, disheveled, needed a shave. "Is this place really free? How long have you been here? You're really not going to charge anyone tuition? If I had only known you were here before this. I was giving away money, lots of money, thousands and thousands, but I didn't know you were here." He paced around, upset. "I don't know why I didn't know you were here. I live right upstairs, you know, and now the money is almost gone, and I didn't know you were here." He was melancholy, apologetic. Hard on himself. "I only have two hundred dollars left, would that be all right?" He left and came back with two $100 bills.

I thanked him. "Thank you so much. Thank you. Thanks. Thanks." I suffered a touch of guilt at taking the last of the man's money, but he so wanted to give it away, seemed so relieved. I ran around the school, hid the bills in the bookcase, under a cushion, in the Band-Aid box, in my bra. I took five children to the sprinkler with two fresh $100 bills finally folded neatly in my blouse pocket. Perhaps the school needed a bank account.

The animals started arriving. Nosy, the rabbit, came from a nursery a few blocks away along with the gerbils, Strawberry, Lemon, and Starfish, and some fish. They were to stay with us for the summer, but no one ever came to pick them up.

Marion's nursery threw out a bunch of big wooden trucks that our children are still playing with.

Jinx bought a large supply of brand-new tempera paints in red, blue, yellow, black, and white and fifteen big thick brushes and several rolls of slick white shelf paper to paint on. Tempera is powder mixed with water and it washes off human skin easily and even out of clothes if the clothes are washed promptly.

One of us had the bright idea of having a pay phone installed. Semi-public classification. 864-9034. Etched into my brain. No phone bills.

The $200 was spent on buying cots for naptime and on getting the phone installed and on some things I can't remember. To keep a small fund for miscellaneous purposes we had bake sales. People would bring food in the morning, the children would do some baking, and then a few grownups and a few children and all the food would go into the center of the Columbia campus around noon and sometimes we would sell out in about an hour and come back to the school with $50 and occasionally we would spend four hours and make $10. Our rule was to raise money collectively. Donations were accepted but not expected. We had decided a long time ago that we wouldn't take up collections so as not to embarrass people, so as not to assume that everybody was middle-class and always had loose money to give away. Hard work with the children was mandatory. Money was optional. People were generous because these were their children and they wanted to give. It was satisfying. In the end the children did help make their own school. They went on scavenger hunts with us. America, the affluent. Lumber was the major thing to look for. But we also found dishes, bookcases, all the tables we needed, a refrigerator, dolls, doll carriages, stuffed toys, and the most exciting find for the children, a broken or outgrown tricycle.

Someone said that a local public school was replacing its first-grade furniture and there was a great rush of Free School people onto the street, but the city garbage trucks got there first and we lost out.

One of the fathers did retrieve a four-by-six-foot green blackboard discarded outside a school, and a year later a neighbor who worked as a secretary at a private school on Fifth Avenue called to offer us a roomful of sturdy wood chairs and desks. Jinx and I made three trips in her station wagon and the children helped unload.

Kathy and Constance were always looking for refrigerator cartons. Kathy walked fifteen blocks up Broadway inside one with only her feet showing because she was alone when she found it and that's the only way she could think to get it up to Free School. A refrigerator carton was great to hide in, to slide down the side of, and to jump on and smash. Constance and Ian's four-year-old son, Edmund, made one into a hotel with two bedrooms with bunk beds, a restaurant, and a library.

The Urban Deadline people left when the major building was over. Ian was still building. He had put out $200 for new lumber and hardware and the proposed kitchen would need shelves and storage and counter space. Jinx said she could afford to be owed the $200 more than he could, so she wrote him a check, and we owed the money to her.

Billy's father built a sandbox to fit in the corner near the outside stairs. That was important to Billy.

Six weeks working every weekend and we weren't finished. One woman said that she was fed up pretending you can start a school without using money. And there was a small consumer backlash. People were tired of laboring for this school, especially the ones whose money jobs were demanding and paid well. It was much easier for them to buy a school than to make a school. Are we saying our children are second class because we are giving them second-class objects? asked one psychologically oriented woman. Our donated objects were often near the end of their life spans and a few days of group use did them in, which depressed us. A few people said that you just have to look at our garbage at the end of a day to know that groups like this never work out.

The children made gallons of paste for their school out of flour and water. Kathy took them to the store to buy the flour, her contribution, and that was their morning project. Demi brought flour and salt from home and taught the children to make play dough. One child inspired two others to join her in throwing cups of flour up in the air. The woman working with Demi didn't like this at all. She aired her feelings at a meeting. If the children were going to participate, if the parents were going to supervise, there would be accidents, there would be wear and tear on the facilities. Factions began to develop over the question of structure—not enough, too much. The complaining woman finally said that she didn't understand why this school was letting such young children have flour. Somebody immediately pointed out that she should feel lucky it was just flour, last week some woman was there proposing they should have enamel paint. Lester defended Demi and the flour. I looked off into space and tried to whistle nonchalantly. Near the end, there were people in both factions muttering under their breaths something like "I can't understand the way some people raise their kids." There was a final voice that said, "Well, anyway, there's ten pounds of play dough in a plastic bag in the refrigerator if anyone wants to use it."

The promised kitchen didn't get installed. The real estate administrators were trying to punish us. Again. They were the owners, the professionals, the people-in-charge, and they always treated us as children, the child-women, the nonowners, the nonprofessionals. Fortunately we didn't see ourselves as children so we refused to be punished or to discuss whether or not we should be.

I was working a thirty-hour week now and I didn't want to spend my weekend organizing a "Give us a kitchen" demonstration. My job was tedious: copyediting a 2,000-page sociological reference work for a big publishing house downtown. Somewhere in those 2,000 pages were at least twelve cross-referenced studies on working mothers, all of which concluded that children whose mothers work are neither more nor less delinquent, neurotic, intelligent, or maladjusted than children of nonworking mothers. One study concluded, encouragingly enough, that daughters of working mothers tended to have higher self-esteem and tended to plan to work on maturity. There were no studies on children of working fathers.

There was also a memorable study in this tome on baby IQs in which the majority of the female babies tested higher than the male babies. From which the studiers concluded that their testing procedures were faulty. The part that knocked my brain around was a whole section of tracts, each of which upheld that old cliché: you can tell the quality of a society by the position, respect, and general treatment given to women and children in that society. And to servants. And to prisoners.

Our demonstration was planned for Monday at 10 A.M. All day the Friday before I was irritated. I didn't want to demonstrate again. I didn't want to persuade or force anyone to do anything. We had taken the storefront only on the condition of getting a kitchen and we had their bloody promise in writing. Resentment was wearing me down. Why should we have to fight so hard to do something so obviously good for children and for the community? By the time I got off the subway to pick up Whitney I was tied up in knots over my imminent responsibility.

Whitney wanted me to see the picture of a tree and grass and a mountain she had drawn using little dots, Roy Lichtenstein style. Whitney had worked on this all afternoon with Constance, and had Scotch-taped it to the wall beside the one Constance made for herself and the one Bootsie scribble-scrabbled. Another rule. The children decided whether their pictures should go up on the wall, not the adults. Demi had made more play dough with the kids. This time they mixed food coloring into the dough, then added yellow to red to see that it made orange, and yellow to blue to see that it made green, and so on. I was trying to get Constance away from all this enthusiastic-child, happy-nursery stuff so that I could complain at length about that damned institution, this damned city, those damned child-hating men, and why did she have to be so damned cheerful when we were about to spend an exhausting weekend planning a damned demonstration?

Constance smiled. "The demonstration is over. We had it this morning."

She explained maternally, as if I would be disappointed, that having it today was only sensible because she and Demi had the kids all day anyway and Demi had a friend who was a politician. Demi called her friend the politician, the politician called her friend at NBC. Constance called whatever parents were likely to be home and after snack the children continued their course work in the urban economics of daycare by marching up the stairs to Low Library to see the president. Again.

The assistant vice-president of public affairs had appeared from his office, made a few nasty remarks to the politician, and stated firmly and pleasantly into the TV camera that the Children's Free School was certainly going to receive a kitchen, had always been going to receive a kitchen. Installation was planned for the following Monday.

The real estate administrators said no. Never. Over our collective dead bodies. The public affairs division had to foot the bill. There was a two-month delay but we got our kitchen.

Such a time would be hard to come by again. The contrasts were startling. For months we had been wrangling with basically hostile officials and punching ourselves around inside the system's paper bag. Now, here we were—out, with our own place. In two or three months, with many people working every weekend and many evenings, the school did get finished. Now it was done: one nursery-type school painted bright colors and stuffed full of too many things.

7.   In the Village:
Money, Rules, Racism, Work,
Fear, Friendship, and the Family

From the day we opened the storefront we were forced to turn away parents who wanted to pay money for their children's care. At our third meeting a few long-time members complained bitterly. Why was our group rejecting parents because they had no time, only money? They themselves had been thinking about stopping their work with the children. Now that we had a storefront, we should hire a professional, someone who knew what she was doing.

Kelley chaired our first meetings. Funding was always first on her agenda. On this night, as we sat in a circle on the assistant vice-president for public affairs' red rug, a few of us on the floor, on the painted milk crates, leaning against the climbing thing, one of the fathers standing, one arm over the trapeze, Kelley insisted we were on our way to becoming a fully financed center for working women's children. Working women had to have funded daycare so we had to get funding. Although Kelley spoke unemotionally, her underlying message got through: Women without full-time jobs should not provide child care for themselves—that was a superfluous activity—when so many women had *real needs* for child care.

Idine was listening to Kelley, agreeing with Kelley, and I was watching Idine, trying not to feel guilty. Idine had *real needs*. She was from Jamaica in the West Indies, the niece of a woman who had been helped by the now-defunct Community Action Committee. She and her two children lived with the aunt in a room-and-a-half in Harlem. She had waited for months for us to get the storefront. Now she could work. She put her children here because her aunt knew us and trusted us to be kind and to feed the children well. Idine's earnings were small and her day's work in the group made the weekly earnings smaller.

I heard Lester's voice, angry but calm. "I didn't think we were going to make a place where a parent could dump a kid and leave."

Kelley's eyes widened. She shuffled the papers on her lap. "The parents are always going to be in charge. Funding won't change that. It will just allow some other kinds of parents to be in the school. Any parent who wants to work with the children *can*."

Because Ian was a practical man, he was in favor of funding. The more money, the better. He had spent the meeting time fixing the bathroom faucet, periodically darting about the outskirts of the circle, delivering one-liners. His last was "Don't be foolish. Surely you don't expect anyone to give you money to take care of your own children."

Kelley knew that Lester and I were against funding. She ignored Ian and asked for volunteers who would fund-raise. Jinx and Demi volunteered hesitantly and then decided they couldn't get together for their first meeting because they were going to their country homes for the summer.

I was worried about the group's exhausting itself trying to raise money and I said so. Three or four of us wanted child care taken out of the commodity market forever. Taking care of children should be something that people did, not something they bought.

Lester asked a question. "If we as mothers and fathers assumed the roles of institutional personnel, making rules, collecting and dispensing information, collecting and dispensing money, how will the lives of our children be any different from children in other institutions?"

There was silence.

Several of the newer members were growing confused and irritated. Money was good. How could anyone be against money? Maybe this group was too crazy for them.

Demi proposed a way out of our conflict. Since getting funded was a long-term project anyway, why couldn't we give each family an option of hiring, privately, a really good person to work their day, perhaps even another mother who needed the money?

That was certainly familiar; wealthier women paying poorer women to care for their children. Half the people there thought Demi's idea was great. They disagreed a bit over the wage to be paid. But within ten or fifteen minutes two dollars an hour was established as a fair rate.

I was insulted. "Two dollars an hour! I will not take care of these children for two dollars an hour. What I have to offer my child and all our children is myself, my mind, my being, and no one can set a price on that and certainly not two dollars an hour."

Several parents were angry with me, but didn't know what to say.

Our economic backgrounds divided us. Two dollars an hour was a good wage for some of the people there, while others earned ten, fifteen, twenty-five dollars an hour. What held us together was the common experience of raising children. That experience, when turned into an occupation, was given a low status. Because of the pressures on everybody to earn more money, there would be an increasing number of important matters that would prevent parents from being with all of our children—especially the wealthier parents, the more educated parents, and the male parents.

I hated these meetings. The week before we had decided that no one could hire a babysitter to work in the school. This week some of the parents who made that decision were absent, several other parents were there, and we were going through it again, with the same result. We were to go through that again and again every time new families joined the school.

I was tired of talking about money. I wanted to talk about the children. Kay whispered in my ear, "Don't start on the children again. The children are not the problem, it's the grownups." She was trying to get the attention of the group. "I hope everyone knows there is no one to work Wednesday afternoon. Will somebody volunteer?"

Everybody was talking, nobody was volunteering, and the meeting was getting away from Kelley.

She called the meeting to order. "What if we get funding with no strings attached? Would that be O.K.?"

Everybody said it would be fine, Ian said again that nobody was going to give us money to take care of our own children, and Constance and I made suggestions about including working mothers in the group without getting funding. There was no rule that the *mother* had to work. The grandmother or grandfather would be as good a family representative as the mother. All of our children needed older people in their lives and the parents could benefit from the grandparents' experience in child rearing. And we were large enough as a group to take care of two children whose families couldn't work. These parents could give to the children by making paint smocks, repairing toys, buying supplies, doing clerical work, or cleaning the school. Four hours a week of this kind of labor seemed fair. It was all set. Constance, who was in charge of admissions, was going to ask the first two working women on her list to come to our next meeting and tell us about their children. Before she turned any more working women away, she would ask them if there were any relatives who could work for the child.

Kelley was certainly not satisfied. I could see it on her face. Two working mothers. There were, in our city, 10,000 children on waiting lists and an estimated 250,000 who could use daycare.

The meeting was breaking up. Kay was still trying to get someone to work Wednesdays. There was a knock on the door. It was a man who introduced himself as Kodjoe.

He had watched our children playing on the front sidewalk in the afternoons and thought this was a good place for his daughter. Kodjoe was apologetic because his wife couldn't work in the school and asked to work in her place. Four or five women surrounded him, agreeing excitedly. All of our children had live-in mothers, but five were separated from their fathers. Lester was working a session in the school and occasionally Don, and we wanted men to help raise the children.

Kodjoe and his wife were from Ghana. She was a nurse. When I asked her about child rearing in her country she looked puzzled. Her problems with the children had to do with *this* country, not Ghana. In Ghana she could come and go as she pleased and never worry about her children. She left them in her village and whoever was there—other mothers and fathers, grandparents, older children—took care of them. At home no one talked of children as a problem. There were no books on the subject.

"Of course the caretaking is easier there; in case of fire the children can run outside and get away. Here they are locked into the middle of a tall building. Here there are many dangers to the children."

She admitted there were a few people in Ghana who discussed daycare: those who lived in cities, in apartments, those who worked in factories. Industrialization made children a problem.

I knew that an urban American neighborhood would never be the same as an African village. Still, I yearned for the community interaction of a village, for the child sharing of such a village, for the freedom to have children *and* come and go as I pleased without worry.

Structurally, our group did have much in common with a village. We lived as separate familes in separate shelters near to each other; we had a children's shelter within walking distance of our homes; and most of us saw child care as a social responsibility, not as a hired task.

That was our structure during our first winter of shared child care. Now that we were out of our homes we were forced into village child rearing in public before any of us recognized that village child rearing was what we had been doing or what we wanted to do. For one thing, we had no words to talk about it. Village child care, the concept, was centuries old—and revolutionary in our time. The concept was so old and so revolutionary to the current generation that we wouldn't think of using the term "village child care." We said we were a do-it-yourself daycare unit. We said we had formed ourselves into a make-do structure, because we didn't have the money to be legitimate—federally funded, city-certified. We said we were a family-style daycare solution—warm and cozy and supportive, with mommy and daddy, and sometimes grandmother, as the caretakers.

Village child rearing was a dream. We were stuck with reality— a New York City reality. Within three weeks in the storefront the worst happened. The mother in a newly admitted family phoned in at 10:30 A.M. on her work day. "I'm not feeling very good this morning. I'll probably be in next week." Click. We didn't know how to reach her. She didn't have a phone. Who was she? How had she been admitted? Nobody knew and nobody found out.

Until now such an action was inconceivable. We had allowed this woman to become one of us, a woman who didn't know the difference between a mother and a volunteer. Our responsibility to each other's children, our interdependence, our dependableness as child rearers were things we took for granted. Now that we were out of our homes and in the community, the intimacy and reliability of our mothers' group was disappearing and we didn't know what to do about it.

At the next meeting we made a written list of rules. The first rule was that each worker had to be responsible for her scheduled time in the school. We felt the written rule was not protection enough so we selected one woman to be our official scheduler. She would know who was working with the children at all times.

Before a new family was added to the schedule, she would have a talk with them. If the schedule was changed—in case of emergency, if a worker switched days with another worker—the scheduler had to be notified. Our problem seemed to be solved and rather easily.

Mary talked about her daughter. Mary was the same Mary who had advised Nancy and me on daycare, the same Mary who had offered us the use of her credentials as a teacher, as a psychologist. The first month she was in the school Mary had stayed all morning every morning with Melorra. She couldn't leave. She couldn't leave her three-year-old, her firstborn, sobbing like that. When she was ready to leave Melorra, she asked us to give her daughter special attention. All the mothers comforted Mary. We knew Melorra would be fine and so would Mary. We had been through this separation ourselves.

Idine couldn't understand Melorra's crying or Mary's staying. "Are you sure her mother's a psychologist?"

I assured Idine she was. "But right now she's a mother."

Kay and I had been working the first time Melorra stayed alone. Mary thought it had been O.K. Now she looked at us for confirmation. We reported: Melorra cried for quite a while after Mary left, then she was fine until 10:30. At 10:30 she started asking when it was going to be one o'clock. We told her again and again and again and at 11:30 she burst into tears. She knew it was after one and her mother had forgotten her. Kay made a paper clock with hands pointing to one o'clock. She labeled it, "Melorra's clock," and taped it beside the real clock so Melorra could match the hands. For the rest of the morning Melorra was fine.

Jinx suggested Melorra might feel better if she had a dime to call home. From that time on, Melorra arrived at school every morning with two dimes in her pocket, one to call home, and one in case the first one got lost.

Jinx announced she couldn't cope. There was too much confusion in the school, most of it caused by her daughter Amie, who terrified the adults by doing "spectaculars," lying on the floor kicking and screaming the second her mother left. Her twin brother, Nick, was friendly as a puppy; he would go off into the back room, to pull the venetian blinds up and down, or to turn the air conditioner on and off, or to swing in the swing back and forth over a friend's prone body. Amie screamed. Jodi sat with her face to the wall refusing to talk or move. Dylan would hit kids with all his might and then sneak out of the grownups' sight to tear up their favorite things—books. Melorra cried.

My daughter, Kelley's daughter, and Kay's daughter were perfectly content. But so many new children together making so much noise scared the new parents.

In addition to the tears over separation, there was the pinching, hitting, biting, scratching, running wild, and destruction of public property. For the first few weeks in the storefront, Kelley and Kay and the long-time group members had run a rather severe organization, neat as a pin. Then there were so many more of us. And one day, when the children were building highways and moats in the sandbox, the supervising mother allowed two dump trucks to travel through the front door and dump their loads on the red rug by the orange climbing thing. The other parents watched and did nothing. A few days later when three of our babies took a load of library books outside and tore their pages out, another set of supervising parents also did nothing. Parental action barely improved when their precious little ones spent time perpetrating violence on one another. So many new babies taken into the group at once gave us problems beyond our experience. The major one was learning to cope with aggression. Theirs. Ours.

One woman in her apartment had been able to handle seven children, maybe not terribly well, but at least she had handled them. Now the four parents confronted with twenty or so babies racing around the nursery stood around and stared a lot. There were fewer babies per adult, the space was designed entirely for child needs, and its contents were nearly indestructible, so why were we having this problem?

Our old policy—that each woman should take care of all the children the way she did her own—wasn't working. In the privacy of our homes, if a three-year-old even looked as though she were about to tear a book or spill her orange juice on the rug or slug a playmate—by accident, on purpose, no matter—she was stopped. Period. Out in public like this we were paralyzed.

To complicate matters, norms of behavior were up for grabs. And the suspicions of the evil intent of other parents were rampant. Maybe *those people* didn't mind if the children poured the paints down the drain, threw the blocks across the room, or ran helter-skelter brandishing a pair of scissors in their grubby fists. I wanted our newest member, Edith, who had joined because close friends of mine had told her we were a solid fine group of people, to have a good experience with us. But what could she think when her co-worker left eight or nine toddlers outside to come into the kitchen to ask her, "Edith, your son is going to do his bm in the sandbox. How do you want that handled?"

Admittedly, part of this behavior was accentuated because we had the cursed name Free School on the door. Originally the word "free" was used because families wouldn't have to pay tuition and because mothers would be somewhat free of their children. The free school philosophy (originated by A. S. Neill in his school and book called *Summerhill*) was a secondary consideration, but in a short time all these people started free schools, these free schools folded, these people wrote books of their own, and there was a whole free school movement. Being a free school sent us away from what was happening before our eyes with our children. A. S. Neill was a good man with good ideas, especially about being kind to children, treating them like other human beings, and reinforcing all their successful activity. He blamed the repressive, unresponsive, sometimes even vicious adults who used to take care of his charges for keeping them from their natural inclinations to politeness, social harmony, and zesty wonderfulness. But Neill himself was the hierarchical head of a country boarding school in England and his charges were seven- to fourteen-year-olds from wealthy homes, children who had experienced years of repression and who had thoroughly internalized social norms in some twisted manner or another. Meanwhile we were quoting him on what our group should do with a band of two-, three-, and four-year-old walking ids, slam-banging around an urban nursery. In most cases our children had been the pampered only child or oldest child, and in all cases they were barely socialized.

While our children were turning into the kind of creatures that only A. S. Neill could save, we talked. Every possible disciplinary action was discussed, philosophical pros and cons considered, and authorities cited: Should children be allowed to play with sand in the school? With water? With scissors away from the table? Should they be allowed to bite? To fight? To throw objects in anger? Which objects? Bean bags? Blocks? Shoes? Socks? Sand? Where? At the feet? At the eyes? Which anger? Should children be allowed to hit an adult? To bite an adult? To scream at an adult? Should children be allowed to have tantrums? Should adults?

A few parents—the ones who didn't read much and the grand-mothers and the ones with nearly grown older children—were upset with the rest of us. "You're making a mountain out of a mole-hill. You don't let kids act up, that's all." We should have listened.

Margaret had already raised four of her own, so she was certain what to do with her grandson, Brandon, and with all children. She knew children needed discipline. Margaret had natural authority; even Billy had always done what she said. With a sigh, she told us, "I get all the children in shape on my day and then by the next Wednesday I have to start all over again."

Evelyn had been through this with her ten-year-old. For her three-year-old she insisted on limits. Children had to have limits. She gingerly approached the subject of *adult* aggression. By the time her first child was born she had been a kindergarten teacher for years, and such a good one that her friends assumed mother-hood would be easy for her. That switch from other people's children in a nursery that closed at three to being alone with *her* child in a nursery that never closed was as difficult for her as it was for any other woman. Being with your own child stirred powerful and complicated emotions. For most women, that first year—feeding the child every few hours; changing the diapers and looking for signs of sickness in the contents; just spending all that time listening to see if that brand-new baby is still breathing—is traumatic. Evelyn asked us to think a bit about the aggression we felt. Maybe we were more afraid of that than of our children's carryings-on.

Not much response to that. O.K., everybody agreed—but what we were looking for was a simple answer, a new gadget, a new book outlining a new technique, new phrases we could use to transform our children into intelligent, calm, socially responsive, but still lively and creative youngsters without too much effort on our part.

We struggled off and on for years, individually and occasionally as a group, to handle aggressive children with one book technique or another, but the books didn't help us because: (1) they presuppose a terribly mature and dispassionate adult; (2) they disagree; (3) their techniques are hard to remember when someone else's child spits on you or your kid; (4) many of us didn't care to read books; those who did disagreed on which books to read, and even when they did agree they couldn't follow through.

Edith had the best line: "I agree with everything the author says. It's wonderful. It's perfect. But I can't do it."

Even though my new friend Chioma's baby was too young for

the group (still in the womb, in fact), she was interested in our problems. She couldn't understand why Americans read books on babies. There were no child-care books in Nigeria. An Ibo wouldn't write a book on such a subject. That would be as silly as writing a cookbook. Eating and raising children were basic activities, like breathing. Everybody had to be able to do it. Your mother was the only one who could teach you how to be a mother. Her last official duty as a mother was to go for a month to each daughter's home when the first baby was born, to teach her everything she knew about babies. She would calm the new mother and make sure that mother and baby got off to a good start together. Later there was the community: the village community. The parent raised the child to be respectful of that community and respected in it. No debates on the right way, no harangues, no flipping back and forth between techniques. There was one way to raise children: the way everyone always raised children. Maybe Ibo children didn't grow up any better than any other children, but Ibo parents were certainly calmer than American parents, which is what the books kept saying the successful parent had to be—calm. We didn't have that kind of supportive community structure. We were trying for something like that, but our culture was in opposition.

There had been a time when parents were considered good for the child. But now parents are considered inadequate by definition, the mother most of all. As young educated women we had learned this in the universities. Child-rearing knowledge once passed on from elder females to the younger ones is now judged unworthy of attention. Several dangerously well-read parents my age didn't want the grandparents near the children. We middle-class parents who embraced the experts' opinions that our parents had been failures at raising us now found the same sources still making the same judgments on parents—except now we were the parents.

Our small group of women had pooled individual strengths, exchanged, shared, and come out with a greater whole; now we pooled what the individual parent had trouble dealing with in private, got it all together in public, and shazamm: failure.

Perhaps the greatest indictment I can make of my society is that it produces so many adults who are afraid of their children. I saw parent after parent back away from the mean child. The rageful child would slug a playmate, would sling her toys across the room, and the parent would respond by changing the subject:

"Maria, dear, why don't you play with your clay now?" That was the progressive parent. Many parents saw it all and did nothing.

I was sympathetic. There was a limit to what a parent could do for a child. By the time they had lived three years together, most of it had already been done: the move to the costlier home with the extra bedroom; the quieting of neighbors who complained about the child noise; and the constant vigils by which the baby was protected from being harmed by the strangers next door, being killed by the cars, trucks, and motorcycles in front of the house, being the thing that tumbled out of the high window on the first spring day or the thing that was left in during the fire. After all that effort, when this same baby, instead of gratefully turning herself into an angel, showed a baser strain—showed she had to have *even more* from mommy and daddy—well, that was the limit. A parent couldn't do and be everything. Besides, the parent had stronger, deeper, more compelling reasons for staying clear of the child's aggressive periods than any expert or any grandmother could offer for confronting that aggression. The female parent in particular was filled with rage over the impossibleness, the unfairness of the child-care situation, a rage that stayed bottled up, bubbling, with no way out because the rightful target was too big, too intricate, and always moving. The infuriating child-care situation was remote, dispersed. However, the child was right there. The fear was that if mother got involved with the rageful child, said no, stuck it out, maybe the ungrateful child would pummel mother, would kick her, would spit on her, maybe the rage would grow, maybe infant rage was catching, maybe the whole shebang would blow and mother would find herself swinging her beloved baby against the wall.

Seeing the way all the other parents raised their children was helpful. Constance was relieved that so many parents were no better than she was. She watched Margaret and saw that disciplining children was all right, even good. Mildred said sometimes her screaming was effective and sometimes Mary's soft reasoning worked better. Mildred also said she watched Mary all the time to learn how to take care of children. I had watched Edith since Whitney put her name on a list of "People Who Understand Me" in her book, titled *Me*. Eventually we began to respond to questions about how to prevent this or that action in a child, with the same answer. "You say *no*. *No*, you can't hit. *No*, you can't call Edmund 'Edward' if it makes him cry. *No*. Just *no*."

Kay cut through our anxieties with a simple statement: "The rules of discipline are the same for *all people*. None of us would allow another grownup to hit us, spit on us, spill food all over us, call us foul names, tear up our things, whine around us, slobber on us, throw a tantrum, or talk to us in gooey baby talk, so why do we allow our children such privileges?"

"Such privileges" were dangerous. People who got what they wanted by having tantrums, being a bully, or crying when they were three or four or ten didn't stop by themselves because they got older. We all had forty-year-old friends whose parents, whose community, had evidently failed them. As Edith said, it wasn't that she cared that much how her sons handled themselves in first grade, but how they handled themselves when they were thirty and seventy and eighty. We all felt that way and that's what made us different from professional child tenders. These were our brand-new children, this was our only chance to do the right thing, and these particular children were so important to us now and for all their lives that we sometimes became afraid.

Disciplining our children got us more upset than it did them. They expected it, were often relieved. The mother's fear that she might be too fierce or punish a child incorrectly was softened when she realized she could apologize and be forgiven. Two- and three-year-olds were old hands at adult fallibility and didn't hold a grudge.

Edith always said that if the children understood not only that you were not afraid of them, but that you cared how they felt, everything would be all right. And it was. Only it took a long time.

Our problems all came together those first few months in the nursery and stayed with us, some forever. Meetings were supposed to make everything right, but village life was no longer that simple. Several people who would never have considered taking children into their homes were now part of our group. One of them was Carlotta. She had joined, ready to run a school. She came to meeting after meeting and talked about the doorknob on the back-room door. The doorknob was broken and she was upset because no one ever fixed it. She said we needed a chain of command here. We had to set up committees. Maintenance must be delegated, and delegated to someone besides her. Carlotta was insistent and she had staying power. Like the Pied Piper, she led everyone off—

Charlotte and her books.

The children arrange to have Jinx take their portrait.

Kay at the children's meeting.

Angela and baby Joshua
make their paper chains.

Nora comforts Whitney.

Melorra and her Daddy and Don.

Dimitri and Lester.

Margaret's day.

Edith reads to Emily and her son, Benjamin.

Washing Steve's motorcycle.

Most of us.

further and further from what they were actually doing with their children.

People were now bringing in elaborate questionnaires to help process new families. Really good questionnaires whose questions, by their length and scope and very pizazz, would tell new families a lot about this place. So an hour would be spent discussing the merits of a particular questionnaire, of all questionnaires, of the nature of the word "question" itself. Then someone would say that files on our children were more important than questionnaires. Then we would debate that until someone would say that we didn't need files or questionnaires because we were all here and could talk to each other. At this point Kay would nearly always say that since we were here and talking she wanted to know who would come in Friday since there weren't enough people to take care of the children. After a thirty-second pause, during which no one volunteered, someone else would declare that talking to each other was not the point. Questionnaires and files violated the principles of a free school.

That kind of statement always led to an endless discussion. What was a free school? How free should a free school be? Were we a free school? How free should a child be? What was free? No one there had ever actually been in a free school. Only a few people had read about them in books. Several hadn't read the books, didn't want to, and there were a couple of people who said they didn't even want to be free.

Near the end of the meeting Kay would ask again for someone to come in Friday. She would look at the floor, push her blond hair behind her ear, and say aloud to herself that she guessed *she'd* come in. Carlotta would make one more plea for a doorknob committee and then we would go home.

Our rules began to emerge in spite of what we said at meetings that they were going to be, or that they should be. We always did what we could for each family. We had rules that three-children families were welcome, two-children families were welcome, parents with low incomes and no relatives could work half a day and get full-time daycare. We also had a rule that one grownup had to be in the storefront for every five, six, or seven children.

The last rule didn't work with the others. If we admitted two three-children families and five two-children families and allowed four families to work half a day because of need, then there would be too few adults to give the children attention. Our rules were contrary rules. A few families could be admitted on a special basis and then nobody else because the group would be thrown out of balance. Several members couldn't understand balance and imbalance as a policy. Policies were rigid. One woman came to three meetings in a row to talk about the rules. "I don't understand. I thought we had a rule that a family could work half a day and still have their two children taken care of. Idine does that. Now you're saying you won't admit another family on the same basis. That's not fair. What is the policy around here, anyway?" Several of us explained that in a small group like ours—personal, flexible, family-oriented—a set policy wouldn't work. Rules that were forever and that were applied fairly to all comers would be so strict as to limit what we could do for a particular family or so loose as to make group child care impossible, chaotic. What we had to judge was the balance within this particular community of children and adults.

Carlotta was one of the people who couldn't adjust to this way of thinking. She wanted rules that were fair and that were forever and, most of all, rules that were decided by a committee. Real rules. Not rules that just happened. She was disappointed in the group for other reasons, too. She had thought we were going to be better integrated. When Barbara brought her son to a meeting and asked if she could join, Carlotta told her to her white face that we really wanted black people. She started counting heads and figuring racial percentages and possible quotas, and it was hard to shut her up and get on with admitting Barbara. Several of us were consciously trying to use meetings to tell each other about our children. Carlotta would interrupt with her doorknob complaint. In private, Carlotta told me she didn't like to hear stories about the children. She didn't want to say so at the meetings because some parents telling the stories were so cute and so sincere. Stories about the children were a waste of time, though. They bored her and irritated her. "All that talk is just like the silly women at the sandbox and reduces us to their level."

Carlotta was domineering and rude and I didn't like her, but she was smart. She wanted to be in charge of a school. She knew that people who did that talked of important educational topics—money, facilities, maintenance, security, test scores, percentages of children who were one thing or another or who did one thing or another. Carlotta tried every way she knew to institutionalize us, but she failed. When she finally left the school she said we were very sweet with the children, but she preferred a more structured atmosphere where the teachers were real teachers and the administrators were real administrators.

I still have fantasies of Carlotta in the center of our group, sitting neatly and quietly with a doorknob jammed down her throat.

We didn't establish a quota system but we did have definite priorities in admissions. It wasn't the particular children so much, they weren't selected by sex, age, intelligence, or personality; they came with their families. We looked for families now, families with men in them, families with grandmothers and grandfathers, nonwhite families, to form a good community in which to raise our children.

And we had always wanted to share our ideas, our skills, and our hard-won storefront with poorer people.

Most of us hated the expanding institutions on the Heights because they forced the black and Puerto Rican families out of the neighborhood. Racism. None of us wanted to be part of it and we all were. We couldn't get away.

Two black youths had taken Kathy's purse while she played with the children in front of the school. Two black policemen hired by Morningside Heights, Inc., had got the purse back. When she refused to press charges they were furious with her and furious with the school.

To form a link with the black community, I arranged a meeting at the public housing project on 125th Street. The meeting was announced by placing a leaflet under each of the three thousand apartment doors in the eight high-rise buildings. Four people came. Two were white. Their husbands were graduate students, they wanted to join right away, and they did. Two were black, pregnant, working part-time, and had brought their older children with them. One black woman was terribly interested in the school. We called her and called her, but we never saw her again.

My friend Suki, who worked with many black parents in the grade school P.T.A., told me to keep trying to make contact there. Then she gave me the facts. Morningside Drive was white country. Even though black children filled up the park playgrounds, scrambled over the rock formations, and went to the public school at the 124th Street end of the park, they knew to stay off of Morningside Drive. The president's mansion was there and professors' apartments and the office of the institution-hired black police force.

Suki said we'd have to go to the projects several times before we could make real contact. People there were suspicious. Too many promises, and too often the promisers disappeared or turned out to be a front for a poverty funds hustle. For us, another struggle. A struggle we didn't win.

Nonwhite families came into our group on a personal basis, because they knew someone or because they saw us taking the children somewhere, or just because the school was there and it was free.

Brandon came to school, up over the park from Harlem. His mother, Rosalee, and his grandmother, Margaret, shared the work day. They were confident in their ability to raise children well. At meetings they listened to the other parents' problems—with over-active children, with the mess the three- and four-year-olds made, with their efforts to control their own tempers. The two women tried to help.

Margaret was strong. She had raised one family and this was her second. She knew about children. She said some of those nervous Nellies she had to work with, with their first babies and their psychology talk and their fluttering around the place, weren't too good for her grandson, but on the whole everyone was nice and she liked being in charge of the children.

On Margaret's day the little ones played ring toss and volleyball with her, while the older ones carpentered with Ed. Then before lunch everyone had to clean up the school. She had them line up at the bathroom to wash their hands. Then the milk crates were lined up in front of the kitchen counter and they climbed up on them to make hamburger patties.

Wednesday was hamburger and French fry day and the children got seconds and sometimes thirds, but they had to say, "Please, Margaret, may I have . . ." and "Thank you, Margaret." There were no dissenters. If a child was unruly or disrespectful, Margaret took her off to the side for a little talk. She said, "I won't embarrass a child in front of the group but I won't take anything off a child either." Her partner, Mishkin's daddy, Ed, had just dropped out of teaching shop at a local junior high. He had long bushy hair, his hands were sometimes dirty, and he left the room whenever Margaret was putting the children through their paces, saying that if he had wanted to hear that kind of crap he could have stayed in the public schools.

Rosalee liked the school. She hated the public schools. She didn't want Brandon pushed around or tested or graded or stamped, as she had been. "It's good for Brandon to be out in the world, learning to get along with all kinds and types of people, and the level me and my mother have to deal with the people on is O.K." Rosalee grinned. "It's fine because, you know, we don't have to live with any of them or love them."

One of the black mothers told another that the school was interesting. She had never seen white people raising their kids before.

A woman from India who had just joined us spent her first session playing alone with her daughter. No one talked to her. I didn't because I couldn't understand her English and I couldn't pronounce her name, even after she pronounced it for me.

I had tried with Lanre. He pronounced his name for me five or six times. Lawn. Ray. Lawn. Ray. I couldn't remember it. I could not hear that foreign sound. I also couldn't remember what country in Africa he was from. He was getting tired of telling me. Lester said I was making a fool of myself, playing the provincial little girl.

The school's Asian families were hardly recognized as real people. Though everyone knew Vilai was from Thailand, one parent kept saying that she couldn't deal with her because she looked just like a China doll. Several other people called her Eiko, mistaking her for a Japanese mother.

The school's black families did not satisfy the missionary zeal of some of the white families. A few whites kept saying that this was *really* just a white middle-class school, neatly shoving the six black families out of the group.

The white mother who said this most often meant it. She was disappointed because she had wanted to be in a school with *real* blacks. None of the black people here counted to her because they were too naturally hip, or too politically aware, or too unimpressed by whites, or too educated, or spoke too many languages, or had too much money, or took care of children too well. Because these families weren't stupid or dirty or lazy or servile, because they didn't need anyone's old clothes, this woman couldn't accept them. As soon as she recognized a black parent as her equal she disqualified that parent as being *really* black.

In the first month of summer, Idine's sister-in-law came in with her two children and more black families joined with two or three children apiece. Several white families went away to their country homes and there were more blacks than whites in the group. That was when we had the Awful Meeting.

Constance had admitted a white woman and her little girl without getting the group's approval and then the woman turned out to be a racist—not just a simple racist, but according to her work partner, Demi, a classic stereotyped white redneck racist whose actions would have been too clichéd for a Hollywood movie. First, Demi talked to her privately and told her she was wrong, that she had to change her attitudes. She wouldn't. Then Demi talked privately to each white parent in the school. What should we do? Response one: She had to be kept away from the children. Response two: She had to be put out of the group. But how? How would we bring this problem to a meeting, discuss The Problem with—in front of—so many black families we barely knew? And what if *she* came?

I wished the problem would vanish, that the black families and the white families had known each other for years, were old friends instead of strangers—that racism was as socially taboo as incest. Constance and I weren't angry with Demi for not throwing her out on the spot. We identified. It was quite understandable that she should know the woman was a racist and still try to work it out. All of us had been through that kind of private white talk and we were used to letting it pass, changing the subject, walking out of the room, just to keep the peace with our children's grandparents, other relatives, with certain white colleagues, with the landlord.

Mary broke the indecision. She told Demi to get her out fast, and to make sure she knew exactly why.

Demi did. Still, Constance and Demi and I, having been brought up isolated among whites, felt we had to discuss this with the whole group, to hear everyone say for the billionth time that racism was wrong. There was probably more to it, perhaps some hope of being congratulated, being especially appreciated because we were *good* whites.

Constance chaired the meeting; she announced that the last woman she admitted was a racist. The black faces instantly went stony, the eyes intense. No one said anything. Her voice was nervous and too loud. "We didn't suspect anything at first. Then she took the white children off to a corner to read them a story. She wouldn't touch any of the black children. Literally wouldn't touch them."

Then Constance announced that I would tell the group more about the woman. I couldn't believe she said that. I didn't want to tell anybody anything. My chest was tight and my stomach hurt. I could feel the tension all around me, as though we were in a thick soup and couldn't get out.

"She asked me why we had to have so many of *them* in the school." Inside my brain I couldn't believe that I was smiling when I said that. Demi and Constance giggled. I wished I could stop my smiling, stop my talking.

The black people in the room were mute, staring at us. Lester tried to help me, tried to help us all. He was watching Lanre across the circle. Lanre was smoking cigarette after cigarette, half-smoking them and putting them out. I knew my husband wanted me to look at Lanre, too, so I did. Lanre was getting increasingly upset. Of course, I thought, he's from a country where everybody's black and he's not used to lots of racism.

Lester's voice was firm, directed at Constance and Demi and me. "Outright racism is something we can handle. That's not going to be much of a problem for us. Latent racism, unconscious racism, that's where we'll have to concern ourselves."

The three of us denied this loudly. We weren't racists, blatant or latent, and to prove it we recited everything the woman said that was racist.

Somewhere in the middle, I couldn't find Lanre. Then I saw him through the plate-glass window walking quickly away from the storefront. I saw Lester following, stopping him, talking with him. I could see this, but I couldn't let go. There was a purge going on here, a confessional, and I was unable to use the intellectual part of my mind to disentangle myself.

When Lester came back with Lanre we were finishing. "We tried to talk to her, to tell her she shouldn't feel that way. But it was hopeless so we told her she had to leave the school."

None of the black parents said a word. Some of the white parents had blank looks on their faces, changed the subject, hadn't noticed that anything had happened at all.

At home, Lester wanted to know what in the world I thought

I was doing. I felt awful, embarrassed. Still, I had no explanation, I could only say, "I don't know. I got nervous."

Until 3 A.M. I was replaying the meeting, replaying scenes from the past. The childhood scenes were in dreamy color, in slow motion, my aunt jerking my arm nearly out of its socket to remove me from the bus seat I found beside an elderly black man, and then the aunt telling the story and all the relatives laughing . . . laughing at four-year-old innocence. Somebody, big and loving, kissed me, somebody tickled me. . . . The scenes of the past year were in color, hurt my eyes, jumbled, flashed, giving me a headache. The old college roommate that I loved, our daughters crawling around the living room, us discussing adoption, a good choice after the first child. My roommate knew she could never form an emotional relationship with a black child, maybe an Indian child, that was discussable. Adoption had to be white.

Another friend who went south to register voters, who wouldn't stand for injustice, beaten by cops, who went to jail to defend black civil rights . . . My friend who sat with me under a summer tree in a glade where deer came, my friend saying that his dogs didn't like blacks, the dogs could tell the difference, probably by smell. I argued. I used logic. I thrashed around among the bedcovers wearing myself out. Stupid to use logic when everybody is crazy and so nice.

I dragged myself out of bed the next morning, ugly, tense, yelling at Whitney. It was raining. We were late.

I didn't want to see Lanre or Rosalee, who were working. I tried to unbutton Whitney's coat with my back to them. But Whitney saw them. In particular she saw Lanre, saw him for the first time. She was afraid of strange grown-up males, took one look at that one, and started howling. "I want to go home. I don't want to stay here. I want my daddy." I did a comforting mother voice that was so tense she cried louder and louder.

"Whitney doesn't like black people. Whitney doesn't like black people." A child was chanting this from behind a beautifully designed block fort.

I didn't speak or move.

Lanre came over, knelt down, and took Whitney's hand. "She's shy, isn't she?"

I said, "Yes," and rushed out the door, leaving her there in her raincoat, crying and holding his hand.

Constance went to Europe for the rest of the summer. She was afraid the school would fold before she got back.

But she needn't have worried. The summer was peaceful. The children went off to the sprinkler or the pool nearly every day. On our day, Kodjoe and I stayed with them in the park. Kodjoe organized running races, jumping races, and falling down races. The falling down races gave the youngest ones a chance at winning. We ate fruit and cold chicken under the trees, and told long stories during which many of the children fell asleep. We taught them to play hide-and-go-seek and they all insisted on hiding together in the same hiding place. Kodjoe helped the children make a bear trap in Morningside Park. The hole was covered with branches, then twigs, then grass. The children said they were going to catch a bear or maybe a human being for their school.

The group was smaller in the summer, mostly black families. Emotional relationships developed, mainly from child to child and from adult to child and back again. It wasn't simple and it wasn't immediate, but it was the solution. After we had sat the children in our laps, wiped their tears, worried over them, traded possible cures for hitting, bedwetting, shyness, and whining, once those parenting emotions started churning, discussions about racists were impossible. Such an event would never happen again. Any person who showed signs of mistreating any of our children was out.

Emotional relationships between adults took longer, were far more complicated, and were always incomplete, up and down, jagged. Black parents discussed whether or not they should be in a school with whites. Some had a hard time staying because of pressure from friends, or because their parents had said such terrible things about whites, over and over from the time they were born. They found it hard to relate to whites as people, to break that stereotype embedded in their minds.

Vilai broke her China doll image fast. We admitted a new mother in the middle of summer and Vilai blew up at her the first time they worked together. The new woman had failed to consult with Vilai, but had lots of orders for her. Vilai stood her ground and screamed. "You can't tell me what to do. Stop it! I am as much in charge as you are. I am more. I have been here longer than you. I will tell you, if there is anyone to tell." Another time, when Rosalee asked if her marriage had been arranged, Vilai laughed. Her girl friends had advised her to chase a certain man, to make him marry her. There was sadness in their married life. Their first babies had died. He wanted a wife at home. She was ambitious. And then there was her temper.

And so it went. Cultures were different. Families were the same. Parental joys, fears, pride could be shared if the adults could govern themselves, if they could structure a workable community.

Everybody was back for the fall, there were seven new admissions, and Kay said we had to get tough about our rules. She said that on the day Kelley was leaving the city for good. Kelley, who was starting her first year at George Washington University Law School, had brought nearly all of Kelley Marie's toys to the school. All with the original paint, no cracks, no wheels off.

It wasn't going to be easy to get tough without Kelley. By the time Kelley wrote to us, Kay was saying that our group was definitely going to fall apart because we couldn't discipline ourselves. Kelley wrote that Kelley Marie was going to a daycare center in a white clapboard house run by Episcopal nuns. It was a nice place, free-flowing. I missed Kelley and I was jealous. I wished that Whitney were being cheerful and free-flowing, someplace away from me. Now that we had admitted so many new families for the fall, I felt responsible not only for Whitney, but for a lot of other children—and adults.

The Spanish-speaking woman whose little girl we had been taking care of for the past three weeks hadn't shown up to work once. I told her she had to work one day in the school. She said yes, emphatically, absolutely, yes. Kay had told her. Yes. Yes. Of course she would be there. Now she said her job was rigidly scheduled, no time off. She hadn't heard us. We were the admitting officials. She needed daycare. So whatever we said, she said yes. And if that didn't work she said she didn't understand. Her need was greater than most of ours, yet we had to tell her we were unable to care for her child without her. We were learning, by experience, that a daycare alternative was different from a daycare solution.

We knew we had to be explicit about our rules, quick and tough in stopping negligence. But making demands on new families was difficult. Direct contact of this kind was socially embarrassing. It would have been far easier to send them a memo, a registered letter, a pink slip. I insisted that some people just didn't understand our group because this society hadn't prepared them to share work, to work when there was no boss and no paycheck.

Kay said that they understood. She and I had always understood and they understood too.

At the next meeting the scheduler resigned her job, announced she was leaving the group, and left. She was quitting from exhaustion. She made her exit line seething in anger. "Groups like this sound good, but they never work because people won't do their share and I am not about to sacrifice my child in the process." No one could talk her into staying. As scheduler, she had received call after call from parents who said their child was sick and they wouldn't be in or that they were sick or that they would be late or that they could only work two hours on Wednesdays or that . . .

Everyone was supposed to find her own replacement from among the other parents and a few people said they had tried or that they had lost their list or that they never had a list or "What list?" They were testing. The scheduler had become the school authority and the workers were seeing how much they could get away with. Our only punishment was expulsion and we were soft on expulsion—tenderhearted. Among the women in our group there was a deep understanding of the hardships suffered by women raising children.

The nursery years were the times when children got sick frequently. It was wearing to make up days missed immediately after being with a sick child, to arrange for babysitters, to pay them. But all of us did this because that was the only way to survive as a daycare group. That was easier to see when there were seven of us, even when there were thirteen of us. Now with twenty-five families—not only mothers, but fathers, grandmothers, grandfathers, and aunts—and a scheduler, it was less clear.

The scheduler had taken her job seriously to a fault. Rather than dump this situation in the lap of the group or tell the persons on the phone they had to work their day or replace themselves with another parent, she had dutifully replaced each delinquent parent herself. It had all become too much. We had a real problem—a group problem.

Immediately someone called for stricter laws, fines, punishments for those who failed in their responsibilities. But that wouldn't help us. A fine wouldn't wipe out the neglect which the children would have already suffered.

The group had become too dependent on the scheduler. We stopped that by eliminating the job. The workers had to replace themselves; that time with the children was theirs. From now on there was no one to call. With no one to call and everyone in charge, the grownups lost their anonymity.

The people working each session were dependent on each other. If a woman didn't do her share of child care she heard complaints from the people on her day and if she didn't act to eliminate those complaints she was out of the group. That expression, "the people on your day," was used constantly. "Do all the people on your day know about Peter's asthma?" "It's up to the people on her day to tell her she can't be late." "Make sure the people on your day know Constance is working for you." We were an oral society again. With signs. One next to the phone listed the times each member of each family worked with the children and noted phone numbers at home and at work. A sign on the refrigerator told about Peter's asthma and that the medicine was inside and the dime to call his mother was taped to the top of the phone. Signed by Marion. A sign on the front door said not to take Idine's daughter to the sprinkler today because of her cold.

Social pressure was more effective than having a scheduler or fines, but it was subject to lapses.

Rosalee saw a mother coming to work two hours late. This woman came in with her son and a container of coffee and sat down to nurse her headache. Just watching this woman made Rosalee mad. She asked me who the woman was and why she was allowed to come at ten-thirty and why she hadn't been to meetings and why nobody said anything.

"The woman's name is Blanche. She's been in the group from the beginning, and I don't know why all this is going on, but I'll find out." I knew perfectly well why no one made demands on Blanche because I was one of the ones who didn't. Four or five of us had mothered her son for the past year and mothered Blanche—getting her a better job, getting her into college, getting her a loan—and as mothers will do, we had begun to look the other way when we couldn't cope with her indiscretions. For the sake of the family.

Last spring Constance had had a public fit about being Blanche's partner. Even then Blanche suffered from headaches. Always. For real. If it wasn't a headache, Blanche was having cramps and their last afternoon together Blanche had gone upstairs to Kelley's apartment and borrowed a heating pad which she laid on the playroom floor with herself on top of it. She asked Constance to keep the children quiet because she didn't feel well . . . which was why Constance had had her fit.

Constance had talked to Blanche a few weeks after we had opened the storefront. She was to come on time. She was to attend meetings. She was to bring projects for the children. She was to set a good example for the families who would be joining us. Blanche's response had been to drop out. Summer was coming and she would take Sean to the sandbox.

She had been back for a month now. Sean looked pale. He had retreated into himself and into his silences, like when he first came to my apartment door. Kay worried that he wasn't being fed enough, so we stuffed him during the school day.

Blanche had already told me her problems. She couldn't possibly get here at 8:30 A.M. to open the storefront. That was too early for her. She had moved to 137th Street. To get to 118th Street on time meant getting Sean dressed and the breakfast made. To drag him that far meant getting up at 6:30 A.M. and she wasn't going to get up then and that was final.

"Blanche, why don't you take the bus?"

"I'm not going to waste my money on bus fare, Nora. I don't have that kind of money to waste."

"Look, if getting up at six-thirty is the only way you can make it here to open the school on time, then that's exactly what you're going to have to do. Worse things have happened to people."

"Nora, you're not listening to me. I said I can't get up that early and I won't do it because I can't."

Blanche had dropped out of school. She was unemployed now. She was soon phoning to ask one of us to take Sean for half an hour after school and then she would show up at the front door at nine or ten, or she would call to tell us she couldn't pick him up at all, to send him home in a cab. She asked Constance if she was interested in taking Sean for a while or adopting him and she asked Kay and Don the same thing. Whether this was serious or whether or not this meant taking on Sean *and* Blanche no one knew.

Constance was waiting for Blanche the next day at closing time.

"Blanche, you can't come to work at ten-thirty and have breakfast. You have to be on time and ready to work so that my children get the same care on your day as I give Sean on my day."

Blanche turned white, was silent, furious. She marched outside to where Sean was playing marbles with three friends. She hit him.

As his marbles rolled down the street and into the gutter, his mother yelled at him, "Where are your socks? You'd better find your socks or I'm going to beat the shit out of you." Sean didn't cry. He was like a stone. His friends—Whitney and Edmund and Charlotte—were frightened. Blanche was out of the school.

Constance phoned Blanche with the names and addresses of three daycare centers in the area. They had long waiting lists but she should get priority because of her extreme need.

When the parents failed in their responsibilities, the children were out too. We were not a school to save children from parents. We were not a children's school at all. We were a family school and I missed Sean.

There had been too many families in and out of the group. We needed stability. Stability was as important to us as it was to any village: common ways, common beliefs, trust. Slowly, by being together, taking care of the children together, meeting together, we developed a body of assumptions we could act on without having to get approval from each other.

Our belief in child care as an activity, not a commodity, was first. And as soon as that was established, Jinx and Nancy both told me privately they were thinking of leaving. Jinx had already enrolled her older daughter in a good private school. She had toyed with the idea of having the twins in the group, but now that the school was definitely free, she felt guilty. She could afford to send her children to any school and although she would miss everyone, especially the children, she didn't feel right taking a place away from some poor person.

Nancy said the same thing. Not that she could afford private schools, but she and her husband wanted the best for their children. Neither of them had been to college and they were willing to make major financial sacrifices to educate Hagar and Bootsie from the age of four and for as long as was needed.

I felt Jinx and Nancy had to stay. Other people could be scheduled into their working sessions, but there was no way to replace Jinx and Nancy's relationships with these children . . . and these adults. The group needed their child-rearing experience, needed their skills.

It wasn't easy to convince them. We live in a society whose people say that money talks and you get what you pay for. If you can't measure the worth of something in dollars and cents, then you can't measure it. The quality of education is equated with the amount of money spent. If a school is free it cannot be as good as one you have to pay for.

And yet we did have to pay—in time, in energy, and in plain hard work. And our children were rewarded. Every week Lester told the children marvelous stories of his childhood in Ohio; Mary taught them songs and guitar strums; Margaret taught cooking on a real stove and she taught the children to clean the school and themselves; Kodjoe had shown slides of Ghana, of his village, of his school when he was a little boy, of his mother with Nkrumah; Evelyn took them to the studio of her friend who was a sculptress; and Joanne wore her nurse's uniform to school and told them about hospitals and gave out tongue depressors, bandages, and bedpans. Joanne's son did somersaults through the center of the group as she talked and then hid under the bed in the library for forty-five minutes. When found he was grinning.

You couldn't buy those kinds of skills; they came with the parent, and only because the parent wanted to give to her child, to the community's children. You couldn't buy those experiences for your child or for yourself. When a family left, the community was changed, skills were lost, life interactions were lost. In a community, unlike an institution, people were not interchangeable or replaceable.

Jinx and Nancy decided to stay awhile longer.

As we talked to each other about our children, about all the things that happened on our day, the happier we got with each other and with the group. Part of the group's recurring anxiety was due to the discrepancy between what we were doing with each other five days a week and what we talked about one night a week. Our activity was 95 percent direct child care, but 95 percent of our meeting time was dominated by administrative wrangling. I wanted approval of a new rule that would improve meetings. For the first two hours everyone would have to talk about their days with the children and only then could a person speak of funding, files on the children, or doorknobs.

My new rule didn't get on the agenda because of a Crisis with the Two Working Women. Lately neither of them was doing any work for the school and they were badmouthing the place to Evelyn and to a couple of other parents. They hoped they could make better arrangements for their children soon, get them in a good school. Their lives were complicated. They already had two jobs, the office job and home maintenance. The four hours we asked of them they saw as a punishment. Cleaning the floors and repairing toys was no substitute for the relationships the rest of us were developing with the children. They were angry at us, and felt deprived. At each meeting they would call us "you people" and ask why we didn't do everything better than we did. Several people tried to impress on them that it was "their" school, too. But they refused to acknowledge that fact. They eventually found other places and we decided to stop admitting any family that didn't provide someone to work during the day with the children.

Once our group was stable, assured of survival, the people in it began listing its faults. The individual dreams of what we were to be had been broken.

We were not a collective. We were not a commune. Everybody did not love everybody else. A few people refused to love anybody. We had not saved large numbers of poor people. The two working women whose children we were going to take care of had been half-expelled. Our child-rearing philosophy—give children love, make children feel good about themselves, teach them everything you know—was noble. However, there was no way to assess the implementation of such a curriculum or to measure the results.

Just after Christmas Nancy left. She had been feeling more and more guilty as the months went by. There was always so much to be done in the storefront and she was unable to give extra time. The new children were so noisy and hard on her nerves. Also, she had been hearing from more and more women that their husbands were going to work in the school and she knew hers wouldn't. That was the situation on the Tuesday afternoon when Constance's son gave Nancy's older daughter a black eye. Nancy's sister-in-law had just arrived to pick up the girls and she was furious with the school because the little boy wasn't punished severely. She had worked in a daycare center where the adults carried switches. Good-bye, Hagar and Bootsie—and Nancy.

With my friend gone, I felt as if my dream of "group" had been broken. Where did I go to cheer myself up? To the Children's Free School. Brandon saw me first. He ran up the block to hug me and kiss me and I heard the other children's familiar chant, "Whitney, your mother's here! Whitney, your mother's here!"

Inside, Jinx was lying on the floor with seven or eight children. They listened to each other's hearts beat. Jinx told them they had lungs in their chests. "Lungs are like two balloons with the air going in and out." Marion's son was outraged. "No. No. No. No. No. No. I do not have balloons in my chest." He trotted his three-year-old self away from these lies. Whitney sat with Demi, who helped her sew new eyes on an old Teddy bear that had been found in the trash and donated by the custodian in the morning.

In the kitchen Mildred was telling Mary about her problems with her husband's grandfather, who was slowly dying in their apartment. And then I told Mary my problems with the school: Nancy was gone for good; somebody had been sick this week and didn't replace herself; and one of the husbands had sat out his session, reading the newspaper, writing letters, and barely speaking to any of the children. Mary patted me on the back. She hugged me.

"You know, Nora, the school will never be perfect. It doesn't have to be perfect. No schools are. Oh, I wish you could have been here today, the children were so lovely. Such a nice day. Did you see Whitney's project? She's been working with Demi for nearly an hour. Oh, have you heard the bad news? Did anyone tell you yet?"

The news about Blanche. She'd had an abortion early the day before on a kitchen table in the Bronx. In the evening she'd phoned Constance for comfort. She was getting a little scared because the bleeding wouldn't stop. The moment Constance actually saw Blanche's blood, she had tried to get her to the hospital, but Blanche refused absolutely. She was convinced that the hospital officials would turn her over to the police and she would rather die than be arrested. So Constance had called in Mary and Demi and the three of them had battled, sweet-talked, and used logic on Blanche. Then they gave her a choice: either an ambulance or the car, and in the next five minutes. It was a long exhausting night. Blanche was still in the hospital—doing fine now. Sean was staying with Constance for a few days.

Mary's good news was really good. Demi had gotten a four-day-a-week secretarial job. The four days weren't part of the original job description, but she confronted her prospective employer with a fiery speech on the importance of group child care. He capitulated, saying nothing much got done on Fridays anyway.

Brandon raced by me into the back room and I followed him. As his grandmother and Idine put away the blocks, the little boy went rushing around, playing tag, ducking, zigzagging, bouncing off the walls. Margaret told him to settle. She told him three more times. "Brandon, I never let your mother run wild indoors, and I won't let you, either." Then she gave him notice.

"Brandon, you sit down or I'm going to beat your brains out!"

Margaret looked at Idine and me laughing behind our hands.

"Well, I *will*. He's been going all day. And then, Brandon, when your mother gets home she won't know where to find those brains of yours."

Brandon sat, sucked his thumb, and watched his grandmother to see when she would forget he was supposed to sit there.

And so it went. There were always a few people who failed to show up for their work sessions. There were always a few people who didn't know how to be with children. But the balance improved. There were more and more families whose members were wonderful with the children and an increasing number of families who stayed year after year. What we had created changed our lives. For four days of the week, every week of every year, Lester and I left our child in the village and didn't worry.

8. Men and Their Babies

The men were on the periphery of their children's lives. Babies were known to be woman's work and most things to do with babies were woman's work. The women were determined to change that. Fathers had to take responsibility for the care of their children if men and women were to exist as equals.

But that's not where it began in our group. We women were not set on sharing the children with men, but instead we had decided to share the men among our children.

In the first few months of sharing children in our apartments we had noticed the effect of having our babies submerged in a female world. The boys were our first worry. Five little boys in our group had fathers who did not live with them. Our group: the eighteen children, thirteen mothers, nine fathers.

Sean would ferret around in our closets and come out in hose and high heels in imitation of the mommies who took care of him and especially of his mommy, Blanche. He would find lipstick and powder and parade around, clownlike, to the delight of the other children. "So what?" we told each other. Of course he's going to imitate the most important person in his life. It's harmless, after all he's only three. Still the scene made us tense.

Billy's response was dramatic. By the time his father left the house Billy was nearly five and already quite manly. He didn't cry at the loss. Innocently, the little boy stopped getting to the bathroom on time and then he gave it up altogether and simply filled his pants several times a day; he knocked Sean halfway across the room when the three-year-old sat in a chair Billy claimed was his. He couldn't understand why the women in the group were so mad at him. He had the same blank look when his mother confronted him about his baby bathroom habits.

Three children had nightmares about all the different ways Billy might hurt them and three mothers called a special meeting to discuss "destructive children."

Billy's mother said we could say anything about him. She knew he was hitting kids and causing trouble. She wanted us to know the home situation—that Billy's life was hard now. Peggy was looking to us for advice, help, comfort. The three women in the group who favored Billy spoke of his intelligence, his tenderness, his vulnerability. That did not satisfy the mothers whose children had nightmares.

We said we would encourage Billy to teach the other children; we would bring in interesting materials for him; we would work with him on a one-to-one basis; we would intervene in his social relationships quickly; we would set firmer boundaries on his behavior; we would sit him in a chair to calm him; we would put him on our laps and cuddle him; we would let him pass out the snack more often. We encouraged his mother to spend more of her afternoon making much of Billy, rather than worrying about her responsibility to the group. All good ideas, but they did not add up to a solution. Billy's life *was* hard and there was no easy answer.

The married women told their husbands about the five boys with no fathers in their homes; about Sean, whose father had never seen him; about Billy, whose father had recently left him. One husband was persuaded to have lunch with the kids on his wife's day and another husband stayed away from work to roughhouse with Billy and Sean. They liked that. Whitney hated it. When the lunchtime daddy was there, Whitney stayed in the back room and ate by herself. And when forced to spend a whole afternoon in the company of the other daddy, she spent it sitting on the floor in a corner, crying. The wife told me this last story. Then the husband asked what was wrong with Whitney; was she getting sick? My daughter had upset them, had made his time with the little boys difficult. I was embarrassed, as if I were the one who had sat on the floor and cried.

Whitney was not getting sick. She cried because she was forced into the company of a grown man and she was afraid. Another little girl had the same fears. She would stare intensely at her feet while backing far away from any man who wasn't her father. We had been dimly aware of the little girls' fear of men for some time but it hadn't been a problem since they rarely came into personal contact with men. A realization: while babies are thought of as woman's work, *female* babies are thought of as absolutely and completely woman's work.

We reassessed our situation. Each woman was asked to add up the time her child was cared for by his father.

There was no time to add up. The fathers did not have the responsibility of nurturing their children for even one hour a week. The fathers were a money source, an occasional playmate. One father did take full responsibility for his daughter every other weekend; a new development, and only because of the divorce.

The married women stopped being do-gooders, a bit piously trying to provide strong father figures for the poor unfortunate little boys. Now we were looking for men not only to father the fatherless boys, but also to father the fatherless girls, *and* to father the boys and girls who already had fathers.

A few months after we opened the storefront we decided that the husbands should work half the family's time in the school—four hours a week. Each child would have more time with her own father and all the children would have access to many different men.

Then the same women who agreed this was essential said they wouldn't ask their husbands to do it: it wasn't practical. Echoing what their husbands had always told them and what their husbands had always been told, they pointed out that men couldn't stay with children because they had jobs.

I was in there fast. "But we make time for the children and we have jobs."

"Yes, but that's different, we're the mothers."

"What's so different? They're the fathers."

The women stared at me.

In spite of previous bravado we were right back to "babies are women's work." We had already upset the social balance by combining our labor. The burden of baby care was no longer on the woman, but on the *women*. Even that change had not occurred without causing some tension in our nuclear families and in ourselves. We were released from woman's plight; we had free time; and immediately we felt—were made to feel—we were getting away with something. Not only by men. Women who sat resolutely side by side at the sandbox watching their separate children—and as Demi said, spent more energy on their one child than she expended on all our children—these women seemed almost fearful of our existence. "Isn't your daughter lonely being away from you all day?" "You mean she's gone all day and you don't have a full-time job?" "Don't you have professional teachers?" "Aren't you afraid something will happen to the children?"

We would explain at length that we did the same things with all these children they did with their own. Were they afraid something was going to happen to their children? What we thought would be impressive was the ease with which we had made daycare for ourselves and the lack of financial strain on our individual families. Still they were deeply into their own social milieu, and though complaining bitterly of the foreverness of their kids, would turn to us as though we had said nothing. "I would go back to work myself, but I wouldn't leave my child with a person I could afford to pay and to get someone good would cost nearly as much as I could make." "Why do you need daycare, anyway? You look pretty well dressed to me." And when we said the men would soon be joining our group, the women at the sandbox said, "Oh, my husband could never do that, he works."

All that was in our heads. There in front of us every day were our children and Billy. We were determined to put these children firmly in the middle of a two-sex world. So we continued with the only means we saw to get men for all eighteen of our children —direct social pressure from wife to husband.

We had married nice men, no wife-beaters or child-beaters here. Just nice college professors, pipefitters, poets, park attendants, Ph.D. candidates, numbers runners, security guards, small businessmen, taxi drivers, and a U.N. consultant. All with the assumption they couldn't work in a daycare center because they had jobs.

In assessing the men's physical capability to work those four hours a week, we noted that college professors and graduate students of the male sex had flexible hours, as did small businessmen, taxi drivers, and U.N. consultants. The security guard had Mondays off, the park attendant various weekdays on a rotating schedule, and the pipefitter quit work at 2:30. Only two men would jeopardize their jobs by spending half a day with the children.

Convinced that he should put in his half day nurturing the children, my husband arrived for his first session carrying three do-it-yourself kite kits. The children mobbed him. None of the kids could put the kites together as Lester had planned. Too young. But they were fascinated by the way Lester could do it. They ran along behind him while he got the kites in the air and then took turns holding the string.

They liked this man. They liked to get him on the ground and crawl all over his chest and stomach. His daughter wanted to sit in his lap all afternoon. Sean and Billy liked to hit him.

Lester was apprehensive. The group might expect him to radiate some kind of supermasculinity. He knew he could never make up for the missing male companionship. True. But being male, he gave of his maleness.

He told the children stories of his nursery school days in Columbus, Ohio. Little Lester stories. There was the time Little Lester sat under the kitchen table, hanging onto the table leg and crying because he didn't want to go to nursery school and the school bus was honking and his parents got down on their hands and knees and were pleading and threatening and pulling on him. There was the story about Little Lester's plan to make a swimming pool out of a hole in the garage driveway. With seven kids working all day it was almost perfect, except for the terrible loss of water problem and the little brother problem. Dicky followed Little Lester everywhere and said everything he said and tried to do everything he did—and Dicky told their father the second he saw him. Just yelled it out. And Little Lester vowed to *get* Dicky but then figured it was no use. His father would have figured out about the swimming pool anyway because he ran the car right into the excavation. Besides his family troubles, there was that bully, Jack Rack, who continually haunted Little Lester's life until one day by the luckiest of coincidences Little Lester managed to upset one of Jack Rack's evil plans and land the villain in the hospital.

Then there were Lester's Super Seven stories, which included such figures as Wrong Way Whitney, Laughing Lisa, Shock-finger Sean, the fantastic fighting Edmund Brothers, and Barrel-chest Billy, who never rested in their continuing fight against the forces of evil. And when all else failed to hold their attention, there was the ever popular Super Baby. This one-year-old female child spent most of her hours sleeping in her crib, but when the need arose— as in the case of parents spanking children unfairly—Super Baby would stand up in her crib, tie her baby blanket around her neck, hitch up her diaper, and exclaim, "This is a job for *Super Baby*."

The men as caretakers of their children seemed to me a perfectly normal—even wonderful—expectation. So I confidently accosted each male who walked in the door of what was now the Children's Free School. The fathers refused to believe I was serious. They acted as if I were merely being sociable—or, to my discomfort, that I was flirting with them. A few men thought I was making fun of them, linking them with little babies. Some men giggled, others laughed good-naturedly.

When one father told me how children were the most important thing in life and how delicious they were, especially at this age, before they learned to think, before they talked, I told him I couldn't agree more. Then I asked him to change his schedule in favor of the children. This man, husband of a professor, looked innocently into my face and talking before he thought said, "Oh, I'd like to, but I have important things to do. My wife takes care of the children."

Three men gave identical statements when asked to work with the kids. "I don't think I could be a mother because I have these other things that interest me."

I was naively incredulous. "But we don't want you to be a *mother*. We have plenty of those. We want you to be a father."

One of the men smiled sexily, "Oh, but I am a father."

All right, he had me. To mother a child was to cuddle, to clean, to hug, to teach. To father a child was to impregnate a woman. The end.

I was asking these fathers to spend four hours a week caring for their children and they were hearing me ask them to change their sex. Men who had their sexuality bound up in their careers and their value on the capitalist market shifted this to their father-child relationships, which they viewed more in terms of money exchange than direct contact.

Constance, handling admissions, stressed the family responsibility and always asked if the father could work or the grandfather. She explained the advantages of sharing the day with the husband, mentioning that one couple was doing that already. Two new women with out-of-the-house jobs persuaded their graduate-student husbands to come in occasionally to substitute for them.

So we had Lester and Kodjoe and Lanre and two more men on occasion. Then Kay got a job teaching in the public schools and we had Don.

With a few men committed to child care we thought it would be easy to get the rest of the fathers into it. It wasn't. One father apologized for not working in the school. He said if he worked in a factory, did a routinized machine job, and got off at two in the afternoon he would be only too eager to come in and be with the children. He looked wistfully away and sighed. "It's hard running a small business. You know, I make my own hours so that's not the problem, but I'm not earning money when I'm with kids and therefore I become less secure. There is always the worry about next year. Will there be enough money?" I heard him say it wasn't his school and he was right though he loved the school; did all the grocery shopping for six months once; got the wallboard and the new tile for the floor; came to the cleanups; and played with the kids when he dropped off his. He would have been the head of the P.T.A. in another place, lauded by all—and we did laud him. Still. There was a group here, raising and educating children. That was the adult function and he was on the outside watching.

Associating child care with lack of money and low status was realistic. Child care *was* a low-status activity. That was because women, who held low status as a group, were responsible for that activity. Or perhaps the circle went around the other way, with women having low status because of their non-moneymaking association with children. It made no difference. The point was that the men knew about these dangers of association with women and children. The final threat: joining the little women would make them little men.

Our children knew all of this at two and three and by five there was never a question or a childish mixup on the way life was.

Whitney organized a fantasy game, saying that Edmund would be the captain of the boat and she would be the captain's wife and tell the captain who could get on the boat.

A continual threat came out of a four-year-old female mouth that if any little boy didn't do what she said, she would turn him into a girl. That would fix him.

Abigail, at five, rushed angrily at Brandon and yanked the toy out of his hand, yelling, "Boys don't play with dolls." Brandon cried. A mother intervened and said that of course boys played with dolls. Boys had to play with dolls, for the practice, since they were going to grow up to be fathers. Then Abby cried.

Abby's mother said there had been a scene at home the night before when Abby wanted her father to play house with her. To get rid of her he had made a big issue out of the fact that boys didn't play with dolls.

I knew Abby's father didn't play with dolls *or babies*. At the last school picnic he sat on the blanket in front of me with his three-month-old while his wife and Abby played soccer some fifty yards away. I watched him sit there calmly reading beside his screaming baby and not touch him or notice him while he screamed. My impulse was to pick the baby up and take care of him as I would his older sister at the school, but I felt strange with his father right there. Finally the mother stopped the soccer game and came to her baby. I would see this mother rushing home from the school at 5:00 P.M., holding Abigail's hand, pushing the stroller. She didn't have time to stop and talk to the other parents. She still had dinner to fix and some laundry to do, and the kids to get to bed by 7:30. Her husband liked a quiet house. His classes over in the early afternoon, I would see him sitting in a luncheonette near my building having coffee with his colleagues for an hour, sometimes two—arguing the merits of the Progressive Labor party and the demerits of all other parties.

After a year his wife came to the school in tears. The money was gone. Even though she never bought anything for herself or the children and the meals she made were so economical as to embarrass magazine editors who wrote up those kinds of menus. Her husband was busing her and the children off to relatives in Vermont.

Not long after they left the city, the father made his first visit to the school. He came to a meeting. Because he was busy, he wanted to be first on the agenda. We sat staring at him as he addressed us as parents. He had decided to do a study on our group and write a paper. He believed he could draw some interesting conclusions. He questioned if mothers were the right people to take care of children since they were not very good at it. Men were much better because they did not have the ego involvement. Several men agreed with him. He was turned down on his study proposal by the women, who, having had more ego involvement with the children—including his—were appalled.

Our group did not lend itself well to studies. Though we had ten fathers scheduled by the end of the second year and all but two fathers committed to child care sessions by the end of the fourth year, Sean and Billy left the school before we could compile proofs of their remarkable change due to the effects of male nurturing. Their mothers' private domestic burdens exhausted them during our first year in the storefront.

Billy's mother, Peggy, was job hunting, and apartment hunting for her nearly ex-husband, and dating, and then she had to spend time at the hospital when Billy had his tonsils out, and then she had mono, and then she found out her nearly ex-husband was living with one of her best friends, and then Peggy fell asleep while she was supposed to be taking care of the children and she stopped coming to meetings, and she was always late for her work session and . . .

Billy did not change. His problems were seemingly accentuated by the influx of new families into our group. Through us he was referred to a psychiatric service. That and the male presence was some help. Lisa's daddy was great with him, just his size and strength placed Billy in perspective. He could easily pick the five-year-old terror out of the scene of combat and remove him, legs still kicking, to a quiet place. Margaret, who had raised one family and was now nurturing her grandson, could handle Billy, but most of the younger women were in daily physical encounters with him in which he loomed larger and larger. "He's only five," I would say at meetings. "He's just a baby." But Billy and Peggy were voted out of the school. One of the fathers called Peggy. She was not at all surprised at the rejection and felt herself to blame more than Billy. She may have even been relieved to have the demands of our group out of her life, but she was also terribly hurt. Billy stayed on for another two weeks while she made arrangements for him to attend a local private school with bells that rang, and a routine in which he knew exactly what was expected of him at every moment. He came back to our group during vacation times for the first year. At his new school things were the same for Billy. He made excellent grades and had trouble with his social relations. When he was seven he said that when he grew up he was going to get married and when his wife had a baby he would go away and leave them both.

By the time Blanche and Sean were out of the school, Sean's interest in female attire was no longer evident. Six months after they left we heard that Blanche was pregnant again. Her doctor at the counseling service tried to get her to accept a hospital abortion because, in his opinion, she was in no condition to care for two small children. Blanche agreed with the diagnosis but refused the treatment. She said she loved little babies. She said little babies were much less trouble than older children. She said she would give up Sean and keep the new baby.

The Children's Free School adults were horrified. The males were the most incensed. Interestingly, all the parents, male and female, directed their anger and sadness at Blanche. There was little thought given to the two fathers who deserted their babies before birth. That sequence of events was also blamed on Blanche.

We are a two-sex species, but few people are up to talking about it. No one wants to say that men make babies. Adults still tell each other that babies come out of women's *stomachs*! In this fantasy, often repeated to children as a significant improvement on the stork story, it is a unisex birth, mother-and-child, with no mention of how this miniature human gets into the female stomach or is to get out of the female stomach, and no discussion at all of why the female stomach is chosen for this lucky honor and not the male stomach, which is biologically equal. Men who reject the stomach story most often connect no namable organs to child creation. Romantically, the infant floats in the hazy magic of a female interior and still comes out *hers*.

Testicles. Penis. Sperm. The words are not unused in our era of sexual liberation, but are more often connected with the male prowess in screwing than the resulting flesh-and-blood child. The fact: sperm comes out of testicles, travels through the penis, rushes into a vagina, onward to the uterus and into the fallopian tubes— where it meets its female counterpart, an egg, and *together* they drift back to the uterus where they grow into a baby. A man *can* make a baby. Because this is so he must be responsible for his sperm. He must also bear responsibility for any child that grows from his sperm.

Blanche, Sean, the new baby, and the long-gone fathers were an extreme case—extreme, but not unusual. Child desertion was an extension of the male non-nurturing pattern. A pattern experienced in our group, as well. A father's presence with the children was a gift that could be snatched away. The women knew this and great efforts were made to keep the men near the children.

A few fathers came to the school and sat down and stared at the children, not having the least idea what to do with them or what to say. I remember incidents of men calling a woman to come from another room to pick up a child who had fallen down. It wasn't uncommon for an on-duty male to look out the window at a child playing on the sidewalk, unattended, and not go outside. Usually the same man would question the safety of the school.

It was hard to say anything to your partner, male and perhaps making $18,000 in a professional position—or just male—when he didn't cook or wash up or tend the crying child. How could one ask a man to spend half an hour of his valuable time scrubbing the spilled glue off the lunch table?

And while the women wanted the men to be with the children, it was hard for some to let them into the female domain. Women resented men who came into the nurturing role so late and with so much male superiority and such different ways of being with children. Lester's stories were considered too scary by some women. Hayward spun the children around too hard and two of them threw up. The men were often critical of the women as being overly protective, repressive, controlling. Women saw men as not taking full responsibility for their actions. Roger didn't ever press the children to clean up. He would sit in the middle of the floor with fifteen children and piles of scraps and bits and pieces and glue and paper and scissors and produce a beautiful, happy, creative collage—and experience—and then take the children off to play, leaving the dregs of the experience in matted gluey clumps for his female partner to take care of. Cleaning the animal cages, the stove, and the toilet was also for the female partner.

And the men stirred up tension among the women. The single women, often, were critical of the men's behavior with the children and they resented the married women's opportunity to share the child-care day with their husbands. It wasn't fair, married women already had it easier than single women, and now this. We re-arranged our schedule. Now, single women with jobs could work half a day—which was unfair to married women with jobs whose husbands refused to have anything to do with child care. To be fair, all the adults should divide the child care evenly. But there were fathers who refused to work and a few more who worked once or twice and then told their wives they wouldn't again—even in an emergency. We were making a change in the social structure and there was no way to make that process fair.

Simultaneously, as we pleaded with our husbands to join us and then grumpily accepted them, we began to depend on their services. It was a continual revelation that men could take care of children.

During a trip to a major corporation we discovered the women's bathroom locked. A crisis. Then Lanre, quietly and efficiently, took all twenty-five children to the men's room. There was elation among the women.

I would look up from reading the children a story and find that Kodjoe had the lunch ready. Being a nurturing father never bothered him at all. But he wasn't an American. He was raised in Ghana. In his village people said the more mothers a child had, the luckier the child. And fathers. All the adults of child-rearing age were called "uncle" and "aunt" by the children and the children expected "uncle" and "aunt" to take care of them. Kodjoe told the men he could afford other schools for his daughter, but he preferred our group because it was a group.

We decided on a new tactic: scheduling all-male working sessions, the men who were natural with the men who were unnatural. It didn't work. We thought men like Lester and Don and Kodjoe would help the other men and also make them feel less lost in a world of women. They did feel more comfortable, but not about taking care of children. The conditioning was deep. The same men still did not play with the children, fix the snack, clean the place or the children. Lester was extremely frustrated. He said the children stayed with him and he had to do everything and he didn't want to work with people who were nothing more than warm bodies. Don said the men were always taking him away from his interactions with the children, trying to engage him in long conversations about anything besides these children. Don said maybe an orientation program would help, but that was nearly impossible because each man was still telling himself that he wasn't really there. It was a temporary occurrence and had nothing to do with children. He was there because his wife was working now and it was only fair that he *help her* with *her* child-rearing duties.

The men's idea that they were only helping their wives was so strong at first that they would think nothing of coming late or even canceling out if something came up. It was the wife who would rush over to the school at the last minute or be on the telephone half the night calling the women in search of a substitute for him.

The men never said they were in the group because the children needed them or because the children were theirs. Bob did. He was a single father. His son had been his sole charge for five years and he readily admitted his resentment at having to take care of him. And now at having to take care of all the children. Not that he wasn't intrigued by our approach to daycare. Educational theory was one of his interests. "The educational essay I can understand, I can discuss it with anyone. It's the children. Just being with them is O.K. *Working* with children is what I can't do. I feel as if I'm navigating a swamp."

Ian said it was like descending from one world into another. He was an assistant professor at Columbia who taught an inter-disciplinary honors colloquium as well as a seminar in Elizabethan and Jacobean literature. He once said unapologetically that he was unqualified to teach in this century because in his day at Oxford they stopped at 1820. With grave doubts about what he was doing in the storefront now that the carpentry was finished, this forty-year-old professor and father of two was a stalwart weekly figure among the tricycles, lost shoes, tears, and baby fist fights. He told his male friends he would give anything to get out of it, but Constance, his wife, was insistent that he stay.

To begin with, taking care of children was such a low kind of work—more suitable for females. He confessed that's where his emotions were, though not his intellect, and he doubly hated being at the school because he continually felt humiliated to be so inade-quate among these women.

The younger the child, the more desperate he felt in her com-pany, though he did not avoid the roughest of these relationships. Ian was one of the few fathers who ever changed Joshua's diapers —an experience that he had rarely had with his own children, who were now out of that stage, and which in the case of Joshua made Ian feel heroic and simultaneously martyred. He never stopped complaining to his wife. "What the hell is Joshua doing in school if he needs his diaper changed?" Joshua was there because his big sister was there and his presence was part of our family-help policy. The explanation did not satisfy Ian, for there were two more important thoughts behind his statement: "If Joshua is so young as to need his diapers attended to, why on earth isn't his *mother* around to look after him?" and "I'm not much bloody good at doing this."

In the course of several months Ian discovered one useful activity he could enjoy with the children. By putting various objects in a circle and designing a pattern of physical moves for the child to get from object to object, Ian devised what he called a catwalk. The child would walk the length of a table, leap up onto a trapeze, swing over to the sliding board, slide onto a mat, turn a somersault, climb up a pole, reach out to the top of the climbing thing, crawl across the top of it, climb down its ladder into a wagon, push the wagon with hands only over to a slant board, crawl up the slant board, and stop at the end of the line of children standing on the table waiting their next turn.

Ian whisked Joshua bodily from object to object, and with his hands on Joshua's back and diapered behind gently folded him in and out of the required somersault. Joshua, it was noted in Oxford accents, was particularly good at crawling up the slant board.

To add to the rigors of the game for the older children, Ian, in his dramatic enactment of the monster Grendel from the Anglo-Saxon epic *Beowulf*, would roam the interiors of the catwalk, ready to eat them if their feet touched the floor.

The children looked forward to the catwalk, and if on Monday afternoon Ian sent a substitute parent, they would complain bitterly.

Although the children and the other adults continually expressed their appreciation to him, Ian still doubted his real usefulness to the group. He avoided attending our weekly meetings. He did not see the group as a prototype that could be used anywhere. To him, we were intelligent people making the best of a bad situation. He was intrigued by the school's flavor of socialism, its nonhierarchical structure, its "true democracy" feeling, but he didn't like being an amateur. He believed in professionalism, had a stake in professionalism. But most of all he was a man and he always knew that child rearing wasn't really his job.

The children didn't care whose job it was. They liked the fathers there.

The little girls knocked themselves out playing with the men. Mike was catching them on the slide and soon five little girls were going down on their stomachs, were going down backward, were trying to somersault down, or were asking Mike to catch them as they leaped off the top.

School was the only place four-year-old Susan saw her father. She had barely seen him during her third year and now she saw him for four hours every week. He brought her presents and played with her friends and formed friendly relationships with the adults she knew. His presence was in lieu of alimony payments and infinitely more valuable.

Children were traumatized by divorce simply because they lost a parent. Mishkin and Eban were two of the happiest children a psychiatrist could hope to evaluate. Mishkin's parents shared him fifty-fifty and if there was any fighting it was over who could have him an extra night. Ed was comfortable with children, having shared in Mishkin's care from the time his son was a week old. He would have several little ones assisting him while he rewired the school, while he unclogged the toilets, while he baked health food birthday cakes for Mishkin's birthday. Eban lived with his father, but all his family was in the school. His mother worked there and his grandmother and his grandfather. His great-grandmother picked him up after school and took charge of his school birthday parties.

Times were changing and we were only slightly ahead of those changes. Judy and Alan had already been sharing child care fifty-fifty for a year before they brought their three-year-old into the group. Alan was the most eager to join. He had spent the past few months in a morning play group with four housewives. A miserable experience. He was a teacher who spent his morning writing *and* caring for his baby daughter (a joke I was familiar with) and he had to have that play group. It was important to him —more important than to the four women, who had resigned themselves to twenty-four-hour child care a long time ago. They didn't hesitate to cancel out because of rain, headaches, or relatives from out of town. And they didn't hesitate to fight within the group—especially with Alan. In Alan's version of the story, most of these women had husbands who never talked to them, who were rarely home, and who did not tolerate a critical word from the people receiving their financial support. Real bastards. A couple of the women couldn't get dressed before noon and were depressed rather continually. In his conversations with them, Alan discovered this wasn't a new situation they had married into—their fathers had been exactly the same. Their children tended to reflect this split.

One four-year-old girl psyched him out the first hour he took care of her and with a glint in her eye asked him why he was Kerry's mommy. He said he was Kerry's daddy. She said he wasn't, he was Kerry's mommy, and then she began to chant, "Kerry has a funny mommy. Kerry has a funny mommy." That was it. For the duration of their relationship, she insisted in loud and irritating tones that he was the *mommy*. Alan said maybe she was smart to keep it up. Because if she ever admitted that he was Kerry's daddy, then what was her daddy? Alan was relieved to be out of that group. At last he could work in a child-care group with men.

He and his wife took care of their daughter and of all of our children every Tuesday afternoon and they both had the rest of the week for adult activities and Alan didn't have any battles.

Steve volunteered to come once a week for a year. He was married, young, childless, a cab driver. He let the children help him wash his motorcycle. Afterwards, Jinx would make numbered tickets and the children would line up and count and re-count their numbered order while waiting to go off with Steve on his motorcycle.

We admitted three single fathers and their children: a free-lance writer who made his own hours; a part-time construction worker, who constantly shifted his time of appearance at the school; and a schoolteacher, who made up his time by working in the late afternoon several days a week.

In our fourth year, in a kind of triumph, Gary asked his employer for half a day off to work in his daughter's daycare center. Although his employer said yes, Gary was still in conflict. He liked his job, felt what he was doing was important, and would have been happy doing it fourteen hours a day, seven days a week. There was a team aspect to his work and Gary worried about not putting in as much time as the rest of the team. He wondered what the people at work would think of him, spending all that time with children. People look at you funny. What's wrong with you? Couldn't you get a woman to do it for you?

He couldn't. His wife said she would not take care of him and their child and their house. He said he loved his wife and his daughter and he came to the school and he also took care of Jenny on Saturdays. It was embarrassing for him, telling people he had to take off work for Jenny or that he had to stay with her on Saturday.

Originally, he hated coming to the Free School. Father images from his childhood were imposed on his brain. He knew those images weren't right, not what he wanted for himself, but that didn't help much.

What helped was having fun with the children. Gary remembered some stuff like headstands and cheststands from junior high school and he did that with the children and painted with them, made snowflakes. "Bump your Buddy" was a favorite card game from his childhood which became a favorite in theirs. Finding out what children were like was exciting for him. He liked to compare his view of the children with what people said about them at meetings. He liked to see them change over time. He said he liked the children and then he looked away. "But there's always a tension that this isn't what I should be doing, that this isn't where I should be."

Our children were growing up with a very different image of a father. The biggest part of that image was formed by the men who came to the children's school to spend time with them, to teach them, to care for them.

When a little girl threatened to change Mike into a girl, Mike just grinned. "Hey, that might be nice for a change."

Don praised Jeff for his tenderness with the younger children, for his ability to lead them, to take care of them, to devise fantasy games that they could not sustain without his help. "You're going to be a wonderful father when you grow up."

Ed would tell them, "It's all right to cry. Boys and men feel sad like other people."

A five-year-old boy wanted to tell Lester something. He looked at his feet. Lester must promise not to tell.

"Yes. You can tell me anything. Anything at all and I'll never tell."

The boy shuffled his feet. "Are you sure? Do you promise?"

Lester promised.

"O.K." The boy looked at the floor, embarrassed. "I think I love you."

9. The Last Word on Officials

The district consultant for city daycare was the first official to pay us an official visit. She was a sweet middle-aged woman who sat on a tiny nursery chair with her knees up to her chin and talked to us about better ways to make play dough and about hiring professionals who really knew about children and about applying for government funding. Interspersed with this line of conversation were questions such as: "How often do you meet with *your* parents?"

She was disturbed by Benjamin's bare chest. Benjamin, who at four had an excellent command of the English language, shoved his glasses up on his nose, pulled the elastic waistband of his trousers up over his belly button, and patiently explained the variances of his body temperature. Then, when the official refused to be convinced, he shouted at her, "I can too go outside with just my cape because I have permission from my pediatrician. Ask my mother. Call Dr. Yodajinski." And he ran outside, cape flying.

"Does this school have health cards?"

The adults looked blank, wanted to figure out the right thing to say and say it. I was reassuring. "You can trust Benjamin. He's been in the school for years, so have his mother and father, and we know his pediatrician, and if Benjamin says he can go without his shirt, it's true. Benjamin never lies."

"That's nice. But we find that children don't really know these things."

Constance agreed and agreed. "Now if it was Travis we wouldn't believe it for a minute. Travis is the one over there in the striped T-shirt. Travis is always having fantasies that sound like lies. He will tell you that he can tie his shoelaces, and cross the street by himself, and swim, and now he's telling everyone he's six. Even when his father told Benjamin he was really three, he looked Ben straight in the eye and said, 'Oh, you know my dad, he's such a joker.' "

We all broke up, except for the district consultant.

"Health cards are a necessity in a daycare center. I'll send you the standard form and some materials related to health care." She checked a box on her green form, which was under her yellow form on her brown clipboard. She wanted us to hire a teacher and get funded so we could be officially certified by the city. It would be easier in the long run for everyone, and besides, that's the way it was done.

Lester looked as if he were about to discuss this issue with her seriously, so we hustled her off to see some macaroni and glue collages. She admired these, discussed the merits of flour and water paste vs. Elmer's glue, community paste jars vs. individual paste jars, and tactfully slipped in a reference to Lester's cigarette.

"Smoking in front of children isn't presenting them with a good image. If your teachers want to take a smoke break they should go into the bathroom."

Constance squished her cigarette into a piece of paper, hid it behind the glue, and dragged me into a corner to tell me how silly this was.

"All the children already *know* Lester smokes. They all go to his house all the time. They've known us too well for too many years. So what will we be hiding?"

But none of this was to the point.

We would not learn anything from this woman or teach her anything. Her group was hierarchical, written record-making, money-exchanging, impersonal; our group was circular, verbal, work-exchanging, personal. Her rules worked well or less well for the administration of groups like hers, but when put up for our group, it wasn't a question of whether the rule was good or the rule was bad, in most cases the rule didn't apply.

The question was what would she do to us if we were unwilling to become a hierarchical, written record-making, money-exchanging, impersonal group.

She was a sweet woman, she always liked to help nice groups like ours, but as she told us, she had a job to do.

In response we reminded her once again that even though our structure wouldn't accommodate a full-time teacher, three mothers in our group had nursery teacher licenses. We also said we would get health cards and discourage smoking and fix the plaster and she said she particularly liked the way we fed the children such nutritious food and she would do what she could to help us in our relationship with the city—but we figured she wouldn't do much and she could tell we wouldn't keep our health cards up to date if we even got them, because we weren't a professional organization.

Then, just before leaving, she pulled out her forms. She checked the box indicating she had visited the center. And then she checked the boxes indicating that she was reporting us and our twenty-five children to the Buildings Department of the Housing and Development Administration of the City of New York, to the Day Care Division of the Health Services Administration of the City of New York, to the Fire Department of the City of New York, and to the Sanitation Department of the Environmental Protection Administration of the City of New York. And that was it.

Two days later, before the district consultant's forms had had time to get to the proper agencies, we were visited by two representatives of the Buildings Department. They had a pink paper that said that an illegal daycare center was operating in our storefront. An anonymous caller had notified them that we were illegal because we didn't have their department's C. of O.—Certificate of Occupancy.

The men pulled out tape measures and made declarations: "The back door is four inches too narrow. The front door swings the wrong way. The ceiling measurement is an inch and a half too short. This storefront fails to qualify for our certificate."

Denying their C. of O. to independent daycare centers was a common practice. I asked what we had to do.

The shorter, chunkier, jollier of the two men explained to me about the scale drawings. I showed him the ones Ashley had done. He said they were beautiful, but they didn't count. The drawings had to be done by an architect's office. We discussed the rottenness of making people buy a C. of O. through an architect's office. And after that discussion he decided he liked me and that he would save me a lot of trouble with a little good advice. First of all, we shouldn't rehang the doors or make any corrections until the scale drawings with all the broken lines showing the planned corrections were approved by his office. Second, we shouldn't put out the money for these drawings until the department gave us a list of all violations and the department wasn't allowed to release information on specific violations. And last, even if we made the corrections, the department probably wouldn't give us the certificate, and since it was illegal to operate without a certificate, he was sure the university would shut us down immediately. He was proud of himself for having been as straight with me as possible and he seemed to assume that we would close our doors apologetically and disband.

That was the one thing we wouldn't do. At the next meeting we went around the circle. "Would you be willing to sleep in the storefront to keep it from being shut down?" Constance and I said privately we would go to jail if we had to. But we didn't know where some of the new families stood. Three old regulars were quiet and tense with their "yeses." Then one of the new men in the group, fortyish, balding, and quiet, raised his hand. "I have two questions: When do we do it? And who needs an extra sleeping bag?" We laughed and felt good. Our strength was assured, when and if it was needed. For now we could get back to worrying about Joshua's problems with his new eyeglasses, Brandon's hitting, and the children's interest in death. Lisa had found a dead bird in the park and she and Whitney and Edmund and then everybody had buried it and dug it up and buried it and dug it up and buried it. . . . Mary had found a lovely book about the death of a sparrow and they wanted to hear it again and again. That was as far as we could see to go with their education on that subject. Telling children about sex was easy for most of us. I fairly spilled over with stories of ovarian tubes and swimming sperm, but death . . . death on the lips of a three-year-old made me want to get her started on a really good project with glue and tin cans.

In a few months, when the district consultant's forms had been processed, we began to be visited by a stream of official men.

The firemen looked young in their sideburns and mustaches and long hair. They asked us to put exit signs over the doors, clear and mark a fire exit from our back door out through the basement corridors to an exterior door, buy a hand fire extinguisher for the kitchen, and keep a notebook listing our fire drills. We did.

The sanitation men wore hats like train conductors. They examined our animals. Our five giant African snails interested them the most. A hometown friend had sent these huge, slippery, slimy delicacies to Kodjoe, but he was too tenderhearted to kill and eat them. Instead he bought them a nice tank, put them in the science section, and tended them daily with lettuce and water. Two days later the men returned with a plastic Baggie which they used to confiscate Kodjoe's snails.

The health department sent two men who looked like old high school football players, very clean, balding, and gone to flab. They didn't speak to us beyond giving their department name and inspection number. After counting the children's heads (over thirty count gets one set of rules, under thirty gets another set), they noted all violations and sent us a Xeroxed copy. Violations: plate-glass windows, peeling plaster, water too hot, carpeting on the floor, broken toys, and on and on through fifty more items.

Our district consultant was pleasant over the phone. She asked if we were still opposed to hiring teachers and getting funded and she said that most of the last fifty violations could be disregarded. The rules were being changed. She said she would record our violations as "in the process of correction."

Nobody came to close the storefront. In April the Buildings Department pressed a court case. From our previous meeting with their representative and from information relayed by several university secretaries, we concluded that the real estate offices of the university were instigating a court case against themselves as a last-ditch effort at repossessing the storefront. The charge was against the landlord for uncertified use of the property. The court citation: *City of New York* v. *Columbia University*.

The public relations office, trying to ward off further anti-Columbia publicity, engaged a lawyer who maneuvered to have the case continually postponed. The judge honored his requests for a year and a half and then made a decision: the university must pay a small fine. The public relations office paid. Case closed.

Nothing happened to us or our children because of official rules. District consultants came and went. We were shuffled about the department, carving a solid niche at the bottom of the employee pecking order. No one wanted us on their list. It was so embarrassing: the Children's Free School didn't fold up and disappear after the first year, as expected, or get further into the traditional child-care system. No change at all. There we were year after year taking care of our children with no money, no records, no certificates.

An Epilogue

If I were writing a conventional book on education, here is where I would explain how any child receiving child care in a village such as ours would be tying her shoes at two and a half, doing complicated mathematical equations at four, reading hundred-page books at five. I would describe how various children did these things the "natural village way." I could make a case. It is true. Yet all that would be proven is that some very young children learn to read, add numbers, and tie shoes if the people around them do those things, and if these are generally important activities in their community.

Our children were not chosen. They came with their families, and as village child rearing was in no way a miracle cure for childhood, they turned out like any other group of children. Some could carry a tune, others couldn't. Some ran fast, some ran slow. A few rushed from activity to activity, their behinds barely hitting a chair. One or two had emotional problems. A few learned reading and writing almost before we could teach them. One or two, we were told, might learn everything more slowly than other children. One was in bifocals before he was three. All of them were kind to each other.

As we raised more and more children, we grew calmer, more confident. Each child had her own learning speed, which had to be respected. Mastery was important, that's all. The child who rode off on a two-wheeler at four and the one who waited an extra two years to ride off got the same praise. The praise was not for being a two-wheeling three-year-old or six-year-old, but for being a two-wheeling person. Reading was treated in a similar manner. As each child mastered that skill, the community showed approval, offered to share more and more books. Reading was an important life accomplishment, rather than an IQ indicator or a rod measuring success or failure.

The community was committed to these people who were children. We formed a network of support. The children knew this, trusted it, and were secure. They learned readily, but not because of money exchanges, or adults with certificates, or real estate value, or teaching machines.

One of our new members, Carol, found this hard to believe. All schools talked about their humanistic aspects, but there were always hidden agenda. Success was what counted. We had been around for a few years already by the time her family joined, so we were stable enough, and she saw much potential in us. If we could only pull all the loose threads together, economize, get more scientific, get the latest materials, administer them properly, follow through on their administration. . . .

Every new parent worried over materials. Materials fascinated parents because they all promised to get the very young child from one learning place to another faster. The fact that most of these were adaptations or spin-offs of materials originally designed to help the mentally retarded was obscured or ignored.

I am angry at the grownups who first equated young children with the older mentally retarded, who saw the marketing possibilities there, the nursery franchises, the product lines. I feel a bit sad for the parents whose fears are manipulated, who want to protect their children, who want their children to "do well" in school, to be liked by their teachers.

However, the appeal of specialized learning materials is impossible to combat. The parent or the school can comfortably make a purchase, put the child aside with the material, and not feel guilty about not expending the energy to teach. All further discussion can then center on the effectiveness or ineffectiveness of the product. Teaching is exhausting. The more comprehensive it gets, the messier it gets. And it leaves one full of such doubt. Besides, you can never hold onto the specifics of how the learning is being passed on, the moment when the brain puts certain things together, how many things are being put together, or how that is happening, or how long it will last.

All of this makes me think of Patty Cake. Patty Cake, the only gorilla born in New York captivity, was playing or fighting in the midst of her parents and they both pulled on her until they broke her arm. Her human caretakers whisked her away, nursed her, programmed her into all the advantages, better food, frequent baths, even the proper amount of playtime with a nice white female human, *and* specially chosen creative playthings. She gained weight. She lost fleas. She learned to patty-cake with her nurse. Such success demanded more. The new caretakers were determined to save her from her parents and all that went with them: watery mother's milk, unclean habits, roughness.

One sane male expert said, "No." His reason: There are things transmitted from being to being that we don't know about. That's the advantage and the protection Patty Cake had to have. Of course, gorillas are not children and zookeepers are not teachers, administrators, or merchandisers for preschools. The only point to be made is the value of the sparks between like beings, the importance of vital, rough, loving connections between old and young.

Carol had always agreed with such sentiments. She wanted the village for this, her youngest child—*and* the traditional infant curriculum to get him ready for first grade. She was frustrated in implementing her second desire, yet she didn't want to leave. Two years went by, Alex was going on six, the family was moving to New Jersey—public school, first grade. I wanted Carol to outline the weaknesses of the village system for me. I loved being part of the village with Lester and Whitney. I could see the village was effective in ways that other systems weren't. But I knew it was also a system, not better, only different from other systems. Carol refused to cooperate. "Alex is more prepared for first grade than any of my other children were." When I reminded her of her frustrations, she frowned. "Well, yes. You see, the school prepared Alex, but not in the ways I always supposed a school had to prepare a child. The most important thing the group gave my son was a chance to test himself. When I was a girl, I defined myself by what my parents and my teacher said I was. Alex has already been released from that. It's so funny, my parents always had to remind me, to beg me to speak to guests, to thank them for presents. I did the same with my older children. But here's Alex with the expectation that they would be hurt if he didn't respond, with the expectation that they might want to share experiences with him . . . that in a few cases he might find a friend."

I separated Alex and his experience from the ongoing village process and thought about it. Two or three grownups in the village didn't notice him particularly, some thought he was interesting, and six or seven thought him an exceptional person, doted on each new physical trick, fantasy, or piece of artwork, and each discovery about letters and numbers. Alex had had time to find his space in the community, to find the people, both adults and children, whose personalities and interests blended with his own. He was confident in his power to master a skill. He was sure of his worth. At six, Alex was a person of considerable experience.

Constance and Ian's son, Edmund, got to be six too, then seven. Whitney got to be six. So did Lisa, Devi, Melorra, Charlotte, Benjamin, and Brandon. Nobody left.

With so many grade-school-age children, we had to make changes. Families began grumbling, they didn't want to leave, but they might have to. It wasn't right taking the space that could go to a family desperate for daycare. Besides, what if the children got to be nine and were nowhere near the skill level of their public school counterparts? So we had regular meetings, extra meetings, special meetings. In three weeks we had approved painful village changes. The community was what everybody said was the most important for them and their children, so we started there. Enough people said that they had to have one person in the daily role of teacher in addition to the parents and grandparents. So we hired Kay away from the public school system. That meant tuition for the first time.

Tuition was minimal, evenly divided, and eliminated whenever we had a successful fund-raising event. Still, paying with both time and money was a strain for several families. There were other strains: that role, teacher, came sweeping over us before we were ready. It was as though Kay, our friend for so many years, disappeared inside a magic cloak.

One father said, "The teacher is like the captain of a ship," and left all the child work to her. Several other parents followed his example. Kay was reduced to suggesting at meetings that one thing parents could do was put out the paintbrushes and empty the trash Then there were the superworkers who took the children off fo educational experiences or designed elaborate projects that con flicted with Kay's projects because they never bothered to talk t her anymore. Kay was the same. The children were the same. Bu the adults had a teacher. So they acted weird.

Since we were paying good money for a teacher, several parent pressed us to keep the children in the storefront all the time so they could learn. They also thought we should reduce the family's time commitment to half a day. Everyone at that particular meeting said O.K. And the next week all the fathers stopped working, except the single fathers and Lester. Mary called another meeting to plead with us: "Shouldn't we give some thought to what we're doing? Did we hire a teacher to babysit, to relieve us of all responsibility?" Slowly families volunteered to put in their full day again. In six months it was a rule.

The men came back into the group. But by then the group was having trouble with the women. Having their babies taken care of for three years had effected changes in the women. Constance had finished her B.A., got an M.A., was well into her Ph.D. and teaching Marxist economics at Queens College. Mildred was teaching full time. Vilai was working as a nurse three days a week. Demi was in college administration. Evelyn was teaching full time in a college *and* finishing her M.A. Eiko was working in a Japanese bank. Rosalee had started college at night. Only one or two women were still at home.

Family incomes were up, the children were older, their mothers were as busy as their fathers, and now their mothers' decisions to work or not to work in the school were as difficult as their fathers' decisions had been a few years ago.

For those of us who stayed, the ongoing village life was much as it always had been. We were calmer, but we still worried over our aggressive children, still disagreed about the importance of specialized materials, still worried about reading skills, even after the children were all reading, still had occasional visits from the Buildings Department man, who threatened us because we lacked a certificate of occupancy, and still had a few adult workers who didn't pull their weight.

We never turned into a utopian society, and we knew we never would. That's not why families wrenched their lives around to work that day in the village. There was something beyond the institutional fights and the working out of rules to govern ourselves, and the fights over what was proper education for the young. There was something more, which had been true about us from the first morning we left Whitney, Sean, and Hagar and Bootsie at Kelley's apartment, and it had never changed through all the scuffling, through all the years.

Each child was a special child. The children were linked to us by family ties: mother, father, grandmother, grandfather, aunt, uncle. The children were our children. We were a community. And that made all the difference.